VMWARE WORKSTATION MADE EASY

Virtualization for Everyone

By James Bernstein

Bernstein, James
VMware Workstation Made Easy
Part of the Computers Made Easy series

For more information on reproducing sections of this book or sales of this book,
go to **www.madeeasybookseries.com**

Contents

Introduction

Computer virtualization is nothing new and has technically been around since the late 1960's even though it wasn't nearly at the same level as what we use today, but rather just a way to share computer resources among a group of users. The virtualization technology we use today started in the early 2000s but has advanced greatly since then.

Virtualization is the process of running one or more computers on or within another computer, commonly referred to as the host computer. These virtual machines (VMs) use the hardware resources of the host such as its CPU, RAM and hard drive space. They can also share the host's network connection to get to the internet and communicate with other virtual machines or the host itself.

There are many companies who provide virtualization software such as Microsoft with their Hyper-V platform, Oracle with their free VirtualBox software and of course VMware with their vSphere hypervisor which is probably the most widely used virtualization platform today.

VMware also offers home and small business users a way to virtualize their computers and servers without needing to purchase expensive software and high powered physical severs to run it on. They do offer free virtualization software known as VMware Player which will let you run one virtual machine at a time but for those who want to get a little more serious, they have their VMware Workstation Professional software which will let you run as many VMs as your physical computer can handle.

Even though VMware Workstation is not free, it is still relatively inexpensive for what you can do with it. You can get your own copy for around $200 to install on one host computer. VMware will also have updates to the software that you will be able to install as needed as long as the updates are for the same version. You can upgrade an older version for around $100. If you want to try the software before you buy it, you can use it for free for 30 days.

If you plan on getting into virtualization or have a need to do testing on computers without risking damage to your main PC (host), then this is definitely the way to go and for the home user, you can't beat VMware Workstation when it comes to performance and features. So on that note, let's get virtual!

Chapter 1 – Virtualization Overview

As I mentioned in the introduction, virtualization has been around for some time and the majority of large businesses use it to some degree to save on the costs associated with buying a physical machine for each server they need in their datacenter. Just imagine a huge company like Google with 200 physical servers in a room compared to maybe 20 physical servers running 10 virtual machines on each one.

If you plan on working in the IT field, learning about virtualization and getting some hands on experience will be very beneficial. It's also a great stepping stone to get you a leg up if you plan on working on a VMware vSphere or Hyper-V system in an enterprise work environment.

Virtualization Explained

Since you have decided to read a book on VMware Workstation, then you must be at least somewhat interested in the concept of virtualization. But you might be wondering what exactly virtualization is.

Virtualization, in the IT world, is when you take something that would normally be a physical object such as a computer, server, network switch, storage array etc. and create a virtual or software based version of that object. That way you can take that virtual object and run it on multiple types of hardware and even transfer it between hardware. And when I say hardware, I mean a physical device like a server that supplies the virtual device its resources such as CPU\processor power, memory (RAM) and storage for its operating system and other files.

This process is done by a virtualization layer that runs on top of the physical hardware and is typically referred to as a hypervisor. You install the hypervisor software on to your hardware and then run your virtual infrastructure within that hypervisor. You can manage this virtual infrastructure with a client that you run on your local computer that attaches to the hypervisor over the network. Or in the case of VMware Workstation, a client that runs on the same physical computer as the virtual machines.

There is a graphic provided by VMware (figure 1.1) that shows a good example of how this works. As you can see from the graphic, there is a physical server called the host on the bottom and then the hypervisor sits on top of that. Then within the hypervisor, you have the virtual machines (VMs) which are called the guests that run on that hypervisor (6 of them on the graphic). Then on the VMs, you can install an operating system (OS) like Microsoft Windows for example and then install your applications within that Windows VM as if you were sitting in front of an actual Windows computer.

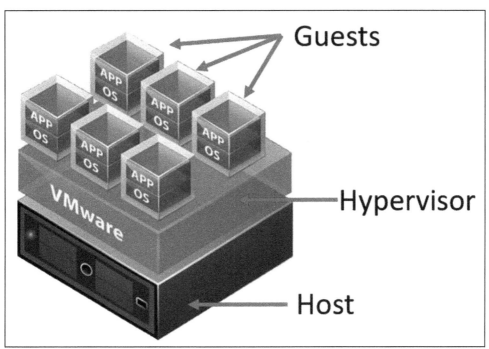

Figure 1.1

The VMs use the server's hardware resources such as CPU, RAM and in some cases, storage as if that hardware was directly attached to the VM itself. This is referred to as shared resources because all the VMs are sharing the same hardware resources. The virtualization resources can even be shared among multiple physical servers allowing you to move your VMs around from host to host without having to shut them down.

Figure 1.2 shows a virtualized environment with three physical servers sharing the same virtualization layer, which will allow you to run your VMs on any physical server without the VMs knowing the difference. This way if you need to perform maintenance on a physical server you can move the VMs that are running on that server to another server while they are still running and then shut down the physical server to perform your maintenance. The moving of the VMs is done over the network that all three servers are connected to.

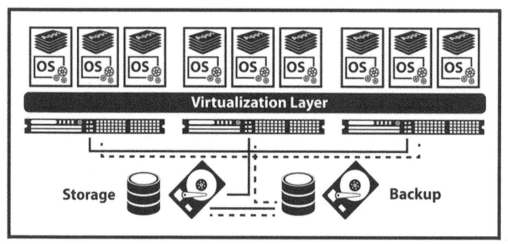

Figure 1.2

This is more of an enterprise level example of virtualization and VMware Workstation does not work quite the same way, but I wanted to give you an example of how a more advanced virtualized environment like you would find at on organization works.

One of the more important things to be aware of when it comes to virtualization is keeping an eye on your shared resources. It's easy to find yourself with slow running VMs because you are low on RAM or CPU power etc. because you are running more VMs than your hardware can handle.

VMware Workstation uses your computer's operating system as its hypervisor and the VMware Workstation software is also installed on your computer's operating system. Plus you manage your virtual environment from that VMware Workstation software installed on your computer. Think of it as an all in one solution on a much smaller scale as shown in figure 1.3. As you can see, we have a computer that can be running Windows or Linux host with VMware Workstation installed on that computer. Then the Virtual Machines are created within VMware Workstation and use the hardware resources of the host that has VMware Workstation installed on it. Then you can install any supported OS that you like on the VMs running within Workstation.

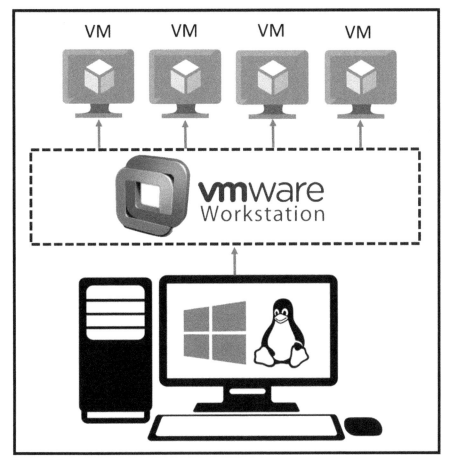

Figure 1.3

Virtualization Benefits
The reason that virtual environments are so popular is that there are so many benefits to having one, especially in a corporate setting. When it comes to advances in datacenter technology, virtualization ranks fairly high on the list of significant innovations.

Cost Savings
One of the reasons for using virtualization for your servers is to save money and we all know how people and businesses like to do that! By being able to run multiple virtual computers\servers on one physical server, it's possible to really

save some money on hardware costs. A typical server can easily cost $10,000 depending on its configuration and if you needed ten servers for your business that would cost you $100,000!

Thanks to virtualization you can buy a super high powered server for let's say $20,000 and run ten virtual servers on it and therefore only have to pay $20,000 in hardware costs. In reality, though you would want to have at least two servers to run your VMs for redundancy purposes rather than having to rely on one piece of hardware running all your servers.

Software companies like Microsoft will also have better licensing deals for their operating system (Windows) when you run them on virtual machines rather than having a separate license for each physical server.

Computer Management

Having all of your computers virtualized also gives you the upper hand when it comes to managing all of your VMs because you can view all of their stats from a central location. All virtualization platforms give you a way to check things such as memory, CPU and storage usage as well as giving you a way to log into the console of each VM as needed.

If you have some VMs that are taking up too many resources on a particular host, then you can move them to another host that has more available resources to even out your VM resource consumption. Many of the higher end platforms can even automatically move VMs from host to host to do this for you.

Experimentation

If you are the type who likes to try out new operating systems and software, then VMs are a perfect platform to do this on. Rather than needing to tie up a physical computer to use for your lab work, you can simply create a VM, install an OS, and then start running your tests.

If you end up messing up the VM, then all you need to do is delete it and start over and it doesn't affect anything in your environment.

Hardware Management

You will see when I get into the process of creating a VM in VMware Workstation that you need to assign hardware resources such as processors, RAM and storage to your VMs in order for them to be able to run. When you are creating VMs they will most likely serve different purposes, so the hardware requirements won't always be the same.

One of the best features of using VMs is the ability to add and remove hardware to a VM as needed. So if you notice that your VM that has 8GB of RAM assigned to it is maxing out its memory when running then you can simply add more RAM to it as needed to fix the problem. Of course you will need to have the RAM available in the physical host to be able to assign it to your VM.

Backups
Backups are a huge part of keeping your infrastructure running reliably. Sure you can back up your files in case you have some type of data loss but what about the computer itself?

Virtualization allows you to back up your computers and servers by either backing up the entire computer itself as a file or series of files or creating what is called a snapshot which is a point in time backup of the state of a particular computer. If you have an issue, then you can revert back to that snapshot and things will be exactly as they were when the snapshot was taken.

Chapter 2 – Installing VMware Workstation

When it comes to software that runs on Microsoft Windows, the installation process is usually fairly easy, especially if you are used to installing programs and apps on your computer. The VMware Workstation installation process is no different and you should find it very simple to install. By the way, you can install VMware Workstation on Linux, but I will be using Windows for my environment.

System Requirements

Just like with most software, VMware Workstation has its requirements for installation that you should check out before you start the process. If your computer is powerful enough to run virtual machines, then it will most likely meet all of the system requirements for installing Workstation. VMware has a nice breakdown of the system requirements on their website so here are the highlights from their site.

VMware Workstation runs on standard x86-based hardware with 64-bit Intel and AMD processors and on 64-bit Windows or Linux host operating systems.

System Requirements
- A compatible 64-bit x86/AMD64 CPU launched in 2011 or later
- 3GHz or faster core speed
- 2GB RAM minimum/ 4GB RAM or more recommended

General Host OS Requirements
- Windows 11
- Windows 10
- Windows Server 2019
- Windows Server 2016
- Windows Server 2012
- Windows 8
- Ubuntu
- Red Hat Enterprise Linux
- CentOS
- Oracle Linux
- openSUSE
- SUSE Linux Enterprise Server

Note that Windows 7 hosts are no longer supported, Workstation 16 will not function on them.

Workstation Pro installation
- 2 GB of available disk space for the application.
- Additional hard disk space is required for each virtual machine.
- Please refer to the vendor's recommended disk space for specific guest operating systems.

Supported Guest Operating Systems
VMware Workstation 16 supports hundreds of 32-bit and 64-bit guest operating systems.

Here is a list of the most popular:

- Windows 11
- Windows 10
- Windows 8
- Windows 7
- Windows XP
- Ubuntu
- RedHat
- SUSE
- Oracle Linux
- Debian
- Fedora
- openSUSE
- Mint
- CentOS
- Solaris, FreeBSD, and various other Linux Distros

For my VMware Workstation host, I am running an Intel I9-11900 2.5 GHz processor and 32 MB of RAM and can run 3-4 Windows virtual machines with 6-8 GB of RAM assigned to each one at the same time so your results will vary based on your host computer's hardware configuration.

Downloading and Installing the Software

If you would like to try out VMware Workstation before you buy it, they offer a 30 day free trail and then you can purchase a license for the software if you decide that you want to keep using it. The license will run you $200 for one host computer. You can download the software for Windows or Linux from the URL below.

https://www.vmware.com/products/workstation-pro/workstation-pro-evaluation.html

After you download the 600+ MB executable file, all you need to do is double click on it to start the installation. The installation process is similar to any other Windows program so if you are used to installing programs then this should be a breeze.

You will need to accept the end user license agreement and if you want to install the Enhanced Keyboard Driver you can check the box next to that option. This will allow keyboard shortcuts such as Ctrl+Alt+Del to work from within the guest operating system without it being intercepted by the host OS

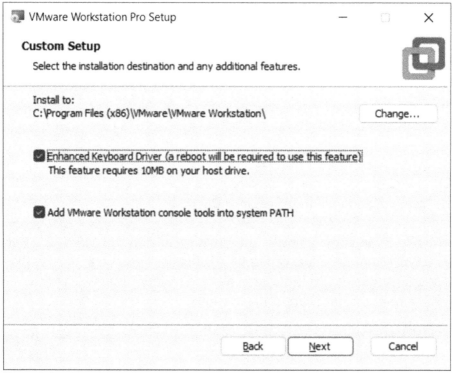

Figure 2.1

You will then be asked if you want to check for updates to the software when you start it and also if you want to join the Customer Improvement Experience Program.

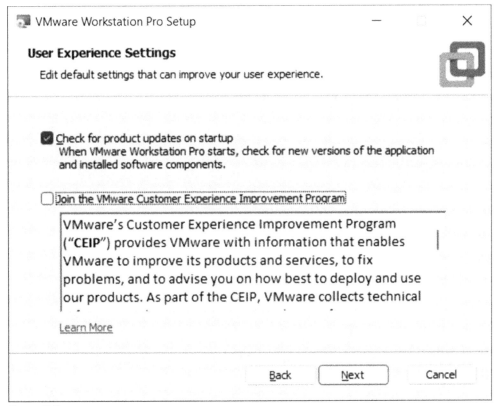

Figure 2.2

Then you can choose to have program shortcuts created on your desktop and start menu.

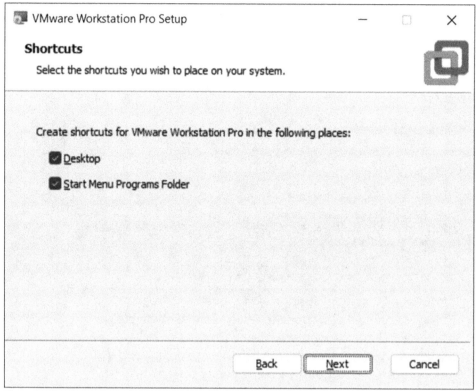

Figure 2.3

Now you can simply click on the *Install* button to begin the installation procedure. At the end you can click on the *Finished* button or the *License* button to enter a key if you have purchased one. Finally, you may be asked to reboot your computer before starting to use the software.

Registering Workstation and Checking for Updates
Just like with any good software, you will eventually need to buy it once the trail period is over. Sure there are perfectly fine free apps out there, but they usually have a higher version with more advanced features that will require buying the software in order to access them. It's kind of like VMware Player vs. VMware workstation where Player is free but if you want all the bells and whistles, you will need to purchase Workstation.

When you open VMware Workstation the first time, you will be asked to enter a license key. If you don't have one yet, you can select the option that says *I want to try VMware Workstation for 30 days*.

Welcome to VMware Workstation 16 ✕

VMware Workstation 16

⦿ I _have_ a license key for VMware Workstation 16:

| -   -   -   - |

Do you need a license key?
Buy now

◯ I _want_ to try VMware Workstation 16 for 30 days

Continue   Cancel

Figure 2.4

If you do decide to buy the software and obtain a license key, you can click on the Help menu and then choose _Enter a license key_. Then you can type or paste in your key to activate the software.

Enter License Key ✕

Enter your 25-character license key.

License key: -   -   -   -

OK   Cancel

Figure 2.5

There is also a registration option within the help menu which is different from activating the software with a license key. Registering VMware Workstation will give you the latest information and announcements about VMware products and services, as well as 30 days of web based support. This might mean extra emails you don't need in your inbox, but the 30 days of support might come in handy if you are new to the software. If you do want to register your software, you will need to create an account on the VMware website if you don't already have one.

One other thing you might want to be aware of is that VMware will have periodic updates to the software so if you didn't check the box to have it check for updates on startup, then you might want to do this manually from time to time. You can simply go to the *Help* menu and then click on *Software Updates* to have it go out and check to see if there are any updates that should be applied.

Chapter 3 – The VMware Workstation Interface

The first time you run VMware Workstation, it won't look too exciting because you will not have any virtual machines configured or running in your environment (figure 3.1). You will see some options to create a new virtual machine or open an existing one as well as connect to a remote ESXi or vCenter server which are the enterprise versions of VMware's hypervisor platform.

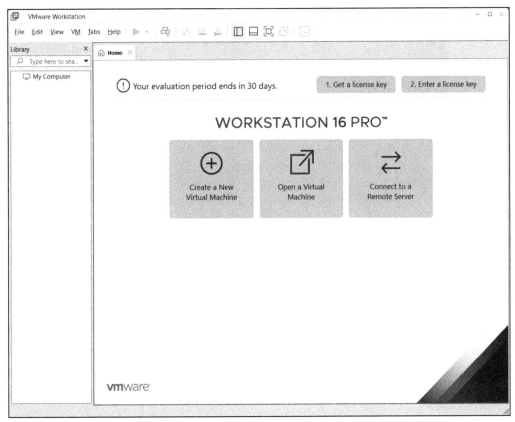

Figure 3.1

Figure 3.2 shows a VMware Workstation environment after there have been virtual machines configured. On the left side of the screen, you have the virtual machine library, and on the top, you have tabs showing which VMs are "open" within Workstation.

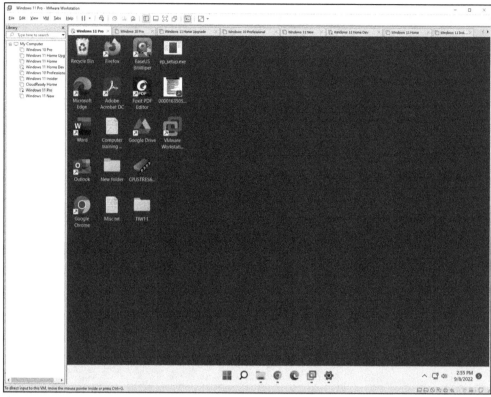

Figure 3.2

Workstation Menus and Toolbar

At the top of the screen, you have several menu options as well as some icons in the toolbar that are used for various tasks.

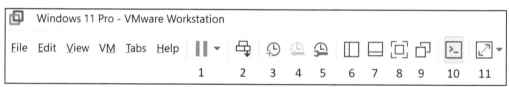

Figure 3.3

I will now summarize what each of these menu items and icons are used for. I won't be going into too much detail because I will be discussing these further throughout the book.

- **File** – Here you can do things such as start the process of creating a new VM or open an existing VM.

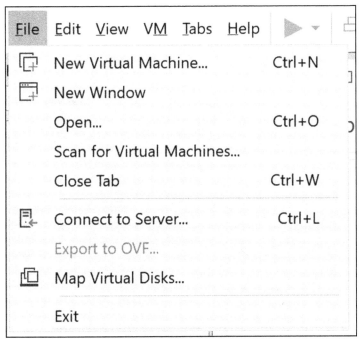

Figure 3.4

- **Edit** – The Edit menu can be used for copying or moving VMs in your library in and out of folders and can also be used to copy and paste text for virtual machine notes such as their descriptions. I will be discussing the Virtual Network editor and the preferences later in the book.

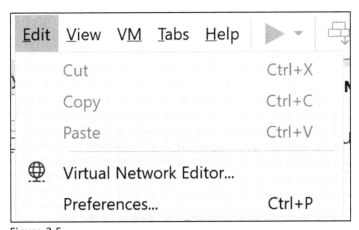

Figure 3.5

- **View** – Workstation allows you to view your virtual machine console screen in a window or in a full screen view which makes it look like you are sitting in front of a monitor attached to the VM itself. You can also do things such as

21

have it fit the current window or stretch the view without keeping the VM's aspect ratio.

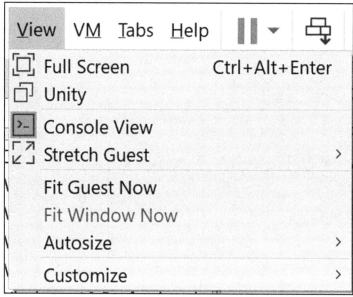

Figure 3.6

- **VM** – The VM tab has many tools for changing power states such as shutting down the guest gracefully or simply turning it off as if you pulled the power plug. You can also use the *Removeable Devices* section to attach hardware such as printers and USB devices from the host computer to the VM. If you want to perform a Ctrl+Alt+Del process on the VM, you can do so from here since pressing these keys on the host will apply it to the host computer itself.

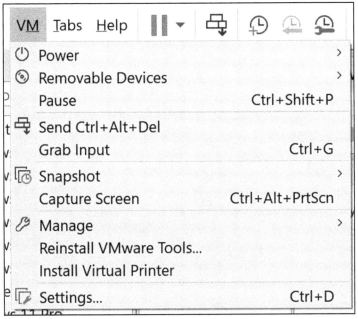
Figure 3.7

- **Tabs** – I'm sure you are familiar with tabbed browsing when it comes to your web browser. Workstation will allow you to have your favorite VMs open in a tab row at the top of the window so you can easily switch between them. More on this later in the chapter.

- **Help** – Here you will find ways to get help when you run into issues. There is an option for online help as well as a way to submit a support ticket assuming you have a support contract. You can also join the VMware online forums where you can post questions and discuss issues with other Workstation users.

- **1. Power State** – You have many options when it comes to the power state of your virtual machines. This section gives you quick access to change the power state as needed. I will be going into more detail about these settings in chapter 5.

23

Figure 3.8

- **2. Send Ctrl+Alt+Del** – As I just mentioned, this will send a Ctrl+Alt+Del signal to the virtual machine.

- **3. Take a Snapshot** – Snapshots are used to create a point in time recovery image of a VM that can be restored later. I will be going over snapshots in chapter 7.

- **4. Revert a Snapshot** – Used to go back to a previous snapshot state.

- **5. Manage Snapshots** – Here you can view and manage your snapshots.

- **6. Show or Hide the Library** – The library is the list of virtual machines on the left side of the window. If you want more screen space for your VM console, you can hide the library.

- **7. Show or Hide the Thumbnail Bar** – The thumbnail bar allows you to have quick access to your more frequently used virtual machines.

- **8. Full Screen Mode** – This allows the virtual machine console to take up your entire monitor.

- **9. Enter Unity Mode** – This allows you to have programs that are running on a VM available to you on your host's desktop. More on this in chapter 8.

- **10. Show or Hide Console View** – This will toggle between showing the console window with or without the virtual machine configuration panel next to it.

- **11. Free Stretch** – If you want to make your VM console window a custom size by stretching it manually, you can choose this option.

VM Library & Tabs

VMware Workstation provides multiple ways for you to work with your virtual machines. Two of the most common ways are by using the library pane and tab rows. Figure 3.9 shows the library pane and my list of virtual machines.

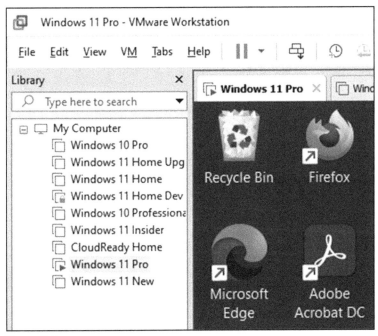

Figure 3.9

The key thing to remember with the library is that it will not necessarily show all of your virtual machines. You can add and remove VMs from your library as needed. When you remove a VM, it doesn't delete or remove it from Workstation or your host computer but simply takes it out of your library list.

You can easily add a VM to the list by clicking on *My Computer* or any blank spot and choosing *Open*. Then you will need to browse to the folder where your VM is located and double click on the **.vmx** file for that particular virtual machine. To remove a VM from your library list, simply right click on it and choose *Remove*.

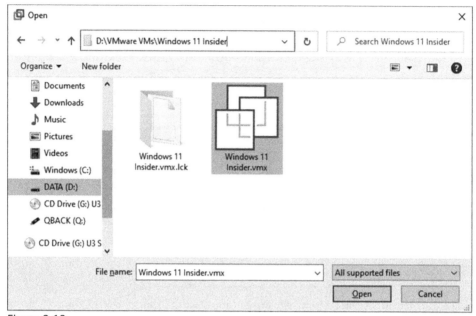

Figure 3.10

Speaking of right clicking on virtual machines, figure 3.11 shows you all of the available options you have when you right click on a VM. Most of these choices should be obvious as to what they do and I will be going over many of them throughout this book.

Figure 3.11

You can also right click a blank area in the library for addition options such as creating a new VM or creating a new folder in the library so you can then organize your VMs by groups. To move a VM into a folder, you can simply drag and drop it as needed.

If you don't see the virtual machine library or accidentally closed it, you can go to the View menu and then choose Customize and then Library.

The tab feature is what I like to use because it makes it easy to switch between your open VMs just like you do with the tabs in your web browser. Then you can close the library window to get more console space on your screen.

Figure 3.12

To open a VM in a tab, you can either double click its name from the library or you can go to *File* and *Open* and once again find the .vmx file for the particular virtual machine.

Once you have your tabs open, you can toggle between them to access your VMs. You can drag and drop the tabs to reorder how they are displayed on the tab bar. To close a tab, simply click on the X on the tab itself.

If a virtual machine is running, you will get a message as seen in figure 3.13. You will then need to make a selection before closing the tab. If you choose *Run in Background*, the VM will stay running but the tab will be closed, and you will need to open it again to get back to the VM. If you do run a virtual machine in the background, just be sure to go back to it and shut it down before you turn off the host computer.

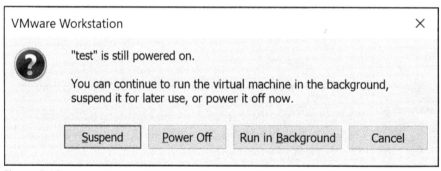
Figure 3.13

VM Thumbnail Bar

There is one other way to manage your configured virtual machines, and that is by using the thumbnail bar. When this is enabled, it will display some or all of your VMs at the bottom of the console and then show a thumbnail preview for the console of each one.

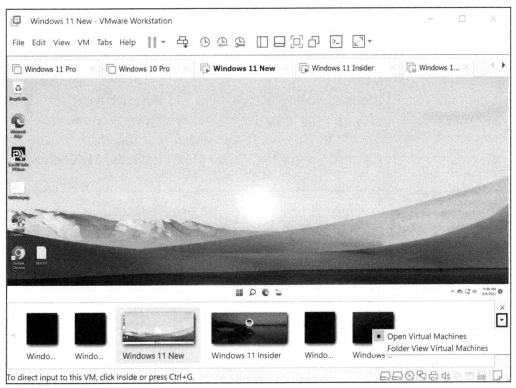

Figure 3.14

Any virtual machine that is not running will be shown as just a black box since there is nothing to see to begin with. As you can see in figure 3.14, there are two VMs running, and you can see their console screen in the preview. Figure 3.15 shows a closer view of these thumbnail previews.

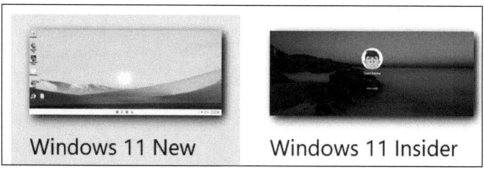

Windows 11 New   Windows 11 Insider

Figure 3.15

At the right side of the thumbnail row, you will see a down arrow (figure 3.14) that you can click to change what virtual machines are shown. You can have only open VMs shown or all of the VMs in a folder within your VM library. If you are not using folders, it will simply show the Virtual Machines under My Computer.

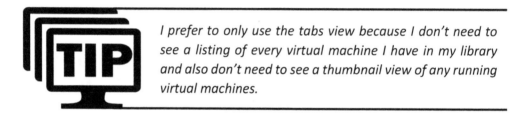

I prefer to only use the tabs view because I don't need to see a listing of every virtual machine I have in my library and also don't need to see a thumbnail view of any running virtual machines.

If you close any particular view and need to get it open, you will need to go to the *View* menu and then choose *Customize* and select the view you need from there.

Chapter 4 - Creating a Virtual Machine

Now that you know how to navigate around the VMware Workstation manager, it's time to get to the fun part… creating virtual machines. The process to do so is fairly simple assuming you know what you are going to be doing with the VM after you create it. Planning this out will help you get the proper hardware configured to get the best performance out of your guest computers.

Operating System ISO Files

A computer without an operating system is pretty much just a paperweight and a virtual machine without an operating system is pretty much just a waste of disk space. So in order to use your VMs, you will need to install an operating system (OS) on them.

Sure you can put your OS DVD in your DVD drive and then attach it to the guest VM, but most people prefer to use ISO files. An ISO file is a single file that contains the image of a disk. Think of it as a zip file that you can mount on a computer and use as if it were another drive. These days, operating system installation disks are in the form of ISO files which are made bootable so you can start the OS installation when you boot your computer.

Figure 4.1 shows the contents of a Windows 11 ISO file. And if you had the actual Windows 11 installation DVD, the contents would look identical.

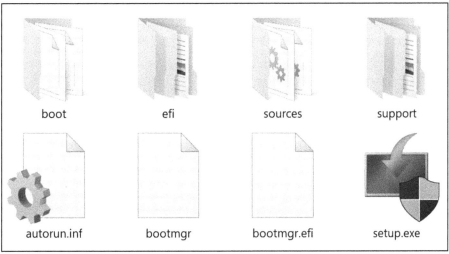

Figure 4.1

You can even extract the contents of an ISO file and then burn them to a DVD or put them in a folder on your computer.

Getting operating system installation ISO files is pretty easy and you can download just about anything online, except for MacOS images since they keep their software locked down unless you have a Mac.

Linux ISO files are super easy to download and so are Windows for the most part. Microsoft likes to change how they do things and it used to be that you would need to run the Windows Media Creation tool to make your ISO file but as of this writing, you can download the ISO file directly from their website.

If you plan on running Windows on your virtual machine, then you can do so without having to buy a copy of the OS. Microsoft will let you use Windows without activating it for a limited amount of time and will then require you to activate it or it will disable some of the features.

VM Storage Location

In order to configure and run virtual machines on your host computer, you will need somewhere to store their disk files and other configuration files. Depending on how you configure your VMs, they can take up a lot of space on your hard drive. I like to have a dedicated secondary hard drive on my host to store my virtual machines since I also use VirtualBox and Microsoft Hyper-V to create VMs.

Figure 4.2 shows the folder containing the files of a Windows 11 virtual machine sorted by the largest files first. As you can see, there are several .vmdk files that are quite large. These are virtual machine disk files, and you can imagine what kind of space they will start to use on your host's hard drive once you start to configure multiple VMs.

Name	Size	Type
Windows 11 Pro.vmdk	73,216,640 KB	Virtual Machine Disk Format
Windows 11 Pro-60.vmdk	34,623,488 KB	Virtual Machine Disk Format
Windows 11 Pro-12916601.vmem	8,388,608 KB	VMEM File
Windows 11 Pro-80.vmdk	266,560 KB	Virtual Machine Disk Format
Windows 11 Pro-90.vmdk	11,584 KB	Virtual Machine Disk Format
vmware-0.log	625 KB	Text Document
vmware-2.log	366 KB	Text Document
vmware-1.log	314 KB	Text Document
Windows 11 Pro.nvram	265 KB	VMware Virtual Machine nonv
vmware.log	249 KB	Text Document
mksSandbox-0.log	55 KB	Text Document
mksSandbox.log	55 KB	Text Document
mksSandbox-1.log	55 KB	Text Document
mksSandbox-2.log	55 KB	Text Document
vm.scoreboard	8 KB	SCOREBOARD File
vm-42.scoreboard	8 KB	SCOREBOARD File
vm-43.scoreboard	8 KB	SCOREBOARD File
vm-44.scoreboard	8 KB	SCOREBOARD File
Windows 11 Pro.vmx	5 KB	VMware virtual machine confi
Windows 11 Pro.vmxf	5 KB	VMware Team Member
vprintproxy-0.log	3 KB	Text Document
vprintproxy-1.log	3 KB	Text Document
vprintproxy.log	3 KB	Text Document
vprintproxy-2.log	3 KB	Text Document
Windows 11 Pro.vmsd	1 KB	VMware snapshot metadata
caches		File folder
Windows 11 Pro.vmx.lck		File folder

Figure 4.2

I like to keep my VMs in a folder called *VMware VMs* on my D drive. That way I know where everything is and it's easy to see how much space they are taking up on my hard drive.

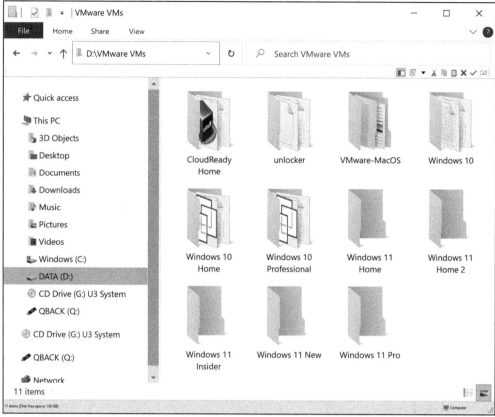

Figure 4.3

There is actually a way in the VMware Workstation settings where you can set a default folder for new virtual machine installations, so you don't need to manually set the path each time you create a VM. I will be discussing this in chapter 8.

Opening an Existing Virtual Machine
You may have a situation where you have a virtual machine on your hard drive from a previous installation of VMware Workstation or maybe someone gave you their configured VM on a disk that you want to import into your environment.

If you have all of the required files for a virtual machine, you can easily open it in VMware Workstation and begin using it. I would first make sure the files are placed where you want them to stay permanently so you don't have to try and reconfigure your VM if you move them later.

There are two ways to go about opening a virtual machine that you have stored on your hard drive. You can open VMware Workstation and go to the File menu and choose *Scan for Virtual Machines*. Then you will need to browse to the folder that contains the virtual machine files and click on the *Next* button.

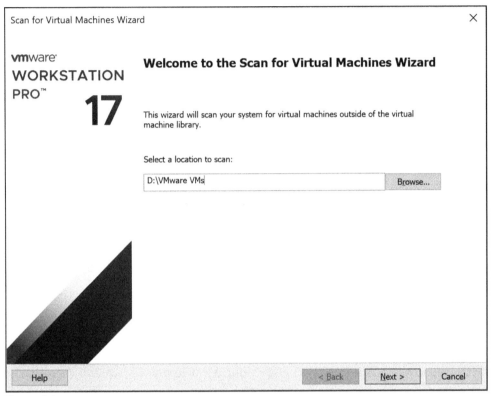

Figure 4.4

VMware Workstation will search the directory you specified for any virtual machines that are not already in your environment and then display what it has found. You can then select the virtual machines that it found that you want to import and click the *Finish* button. They will then be added to your library and you should be able to start them up and make sure they will run properly.

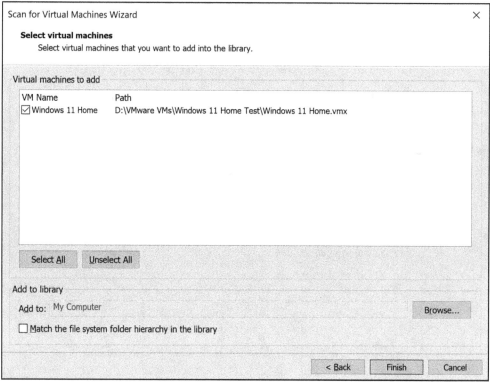

Figure 4.5

Another way to add a VM to your inventory is to find the location of the virtual machine's files and look for the **.vmx** file. If you don't have the option to have file extensions shown in File Explorer, you might want to do that so you can see the entire name of the file.

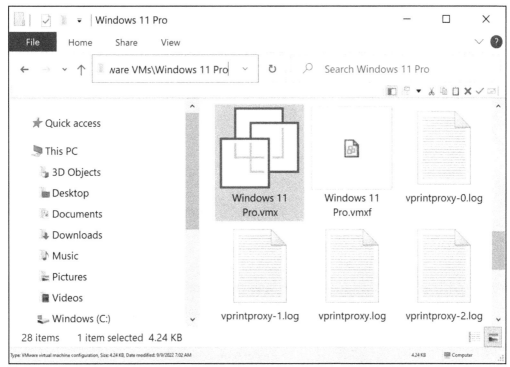

Figure 4.6

Once you find the vmx file, simply double click it and it should open the VM in Workstation and you should be ready to go.

The VM Creation Process
For the most part, you will be creating your virtual machines "from scratch" so it's important to know the process for doing so. There are two methods you can use when creating a virtual machine.

You can start the process from the *File* menu and then click on *New Virtual Machine*. You can also right click a blank area in the library, and you will have the same option.

Once you start the VM creation process, you will have the option to use the *Typical* method or the *Custom* method. I will create a VM using the Typical method first and then the Custom method.

Figure 4.7

On the first screen, I will need to decide if I want to use my host's CD drive for the installation media or I can attach an ISO file to be used to install the OS. I can also create the VM and install the operating system later. I will use the ISO file option and browse to my Windows 11 ISO file.

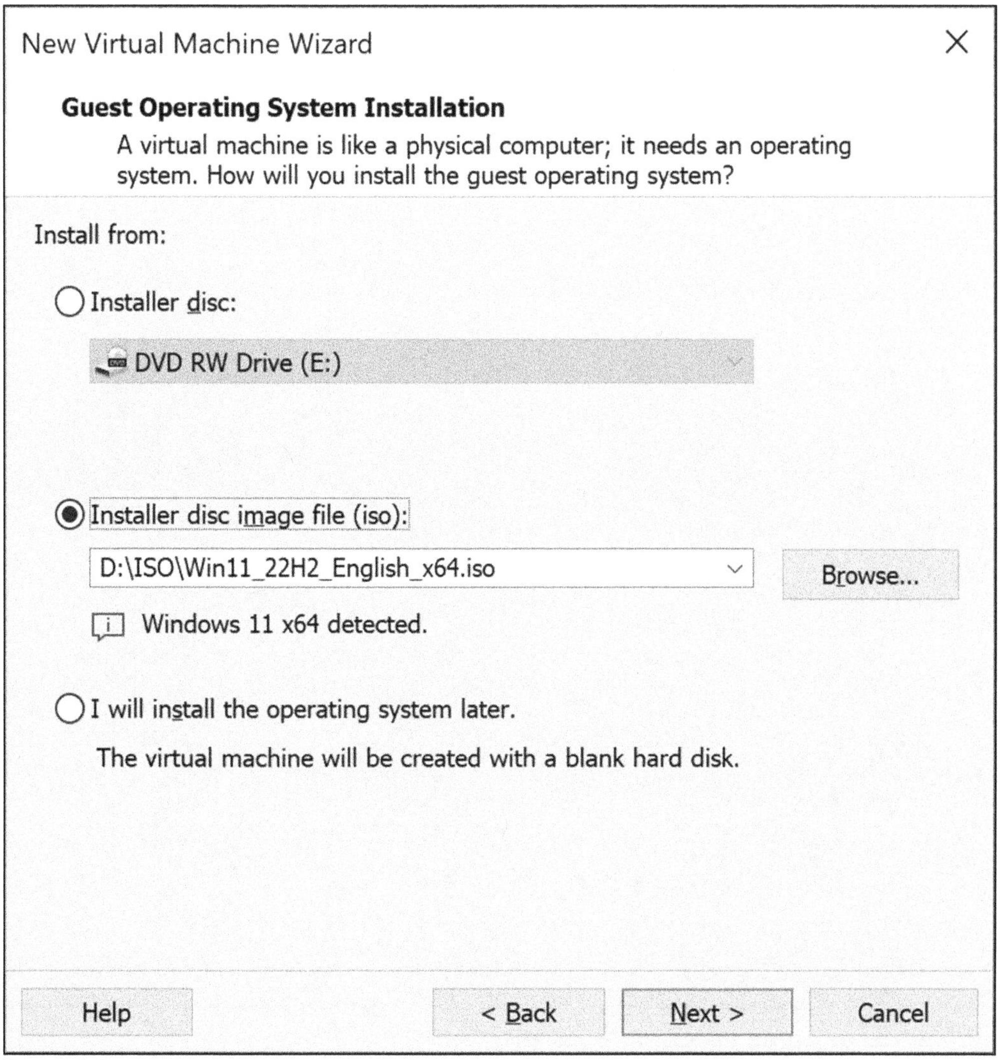

New Virtual Machine Wizard ✕

Guest Operating System Installation
A virtual machine is like a physical computer; it needs an operating system. How will you install the guest operating system?

Install from:

◯ Installer disc:

⊙ DVD RW Drive (E:)

◉ Installer disc image file (iso):

D:\ISO\Win11_22H2_English_x64.iso   ⌄   Browse...

ⓘ Windows 11 x64 detected.

◯ I will install the operating system later.

The virtual machine will be created with a blank hard disk.

Help		< Back	Next >	Cancel

Figure 4.8

The new VM wizard was able to detect that my ISO file was for Windows 11 so it will know how to better configure the OS when creating the virtual machine. If Workstation couldn't tell the OS from the ISO file, I would need to specify the guest operating system in the next screen which will not be shown since it did identify the operating system. Figure 4.9 shows what this screen looks like if I did have to specify an OS to go with my ISO file.

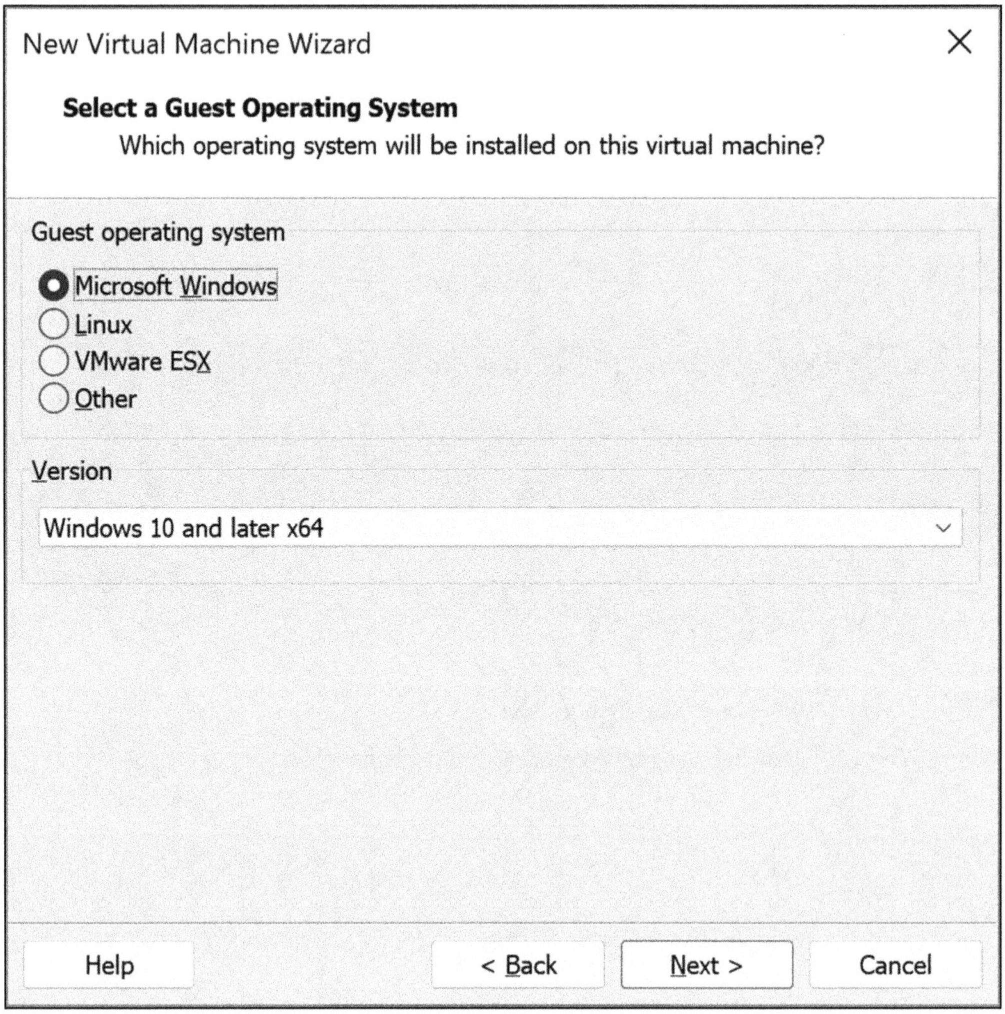

New Virtual Machine Wizard ✕

Select a Guest Operating System
Which operating system will be installed on this virtual machine?

Guest operating system

◉ Microsoft Windows
◯ Linux
◯ VMware ESX
◯ Other

Version

Windows 10 and later x64 ⌄

| Help | | < Back | Next > | Cancel |

Figure 4.9

Now I will need to name my virtual machine and specify the storage location for its files.

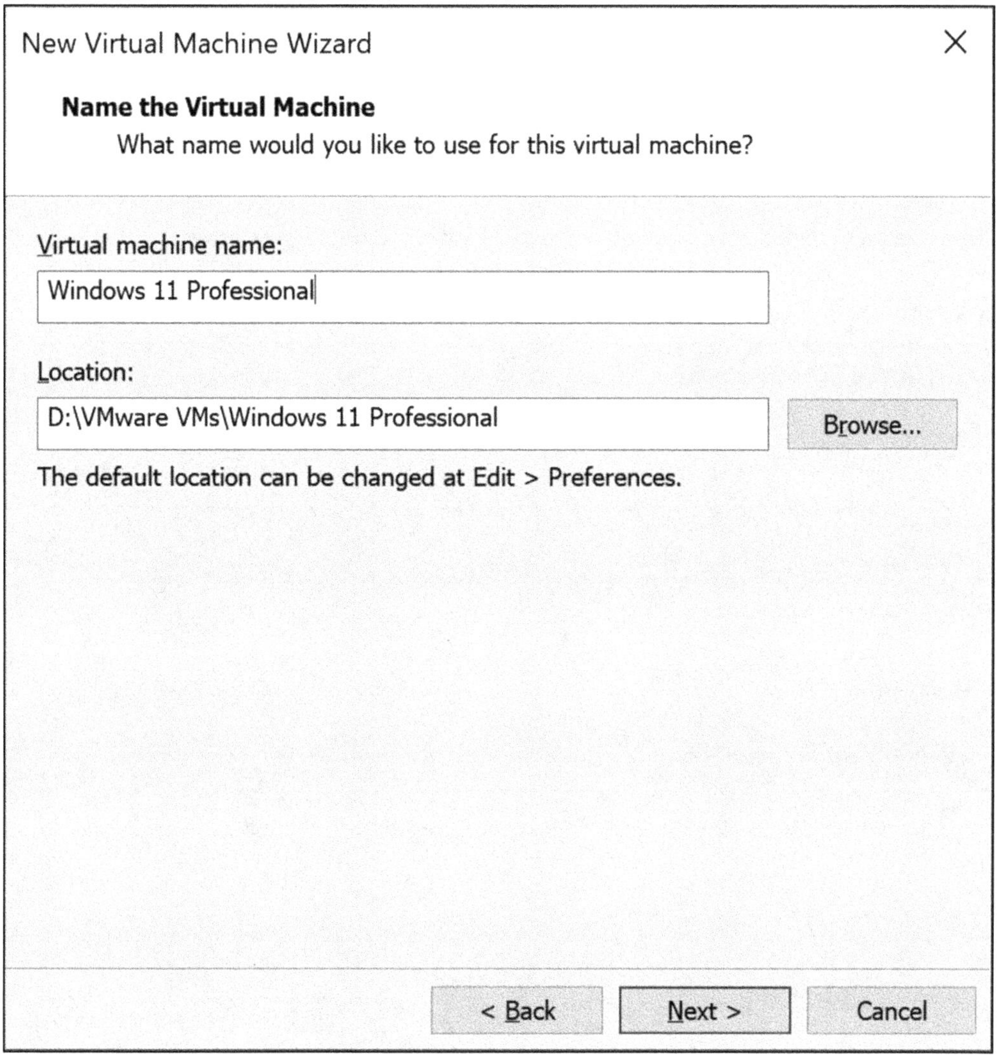

New Virtual Machine Wizard   ✕

Name the Virtual Machine
What name would you like to use for this virtual machine?

Virtual machine name:

Windows 11 Professional

Location:

D:\VMware VMs\Windows 11 Professional   Browse...

The default location can be changed at Edit > Preferences.

< Back   Next >   Cancel

Figure 4.10

Since I am installing Windows 11 on my guest VM, Workstation will want to encrypt the virtual machine's files and install a TPM (Trusted Platform Module) since it's a requirement for Windows 11. This process is new to VMware Workstation 17 and with older versions, you need to encrypt the VM and add a TPM after configuring it and before installing Windows 11.

Figure 4.11 shows how I have the option to encrypt all of the virtual machine's files or just the ones that are required to run Windows 11. I will also need to supply the encryption password and have the option to have it stored in the Credential Manager so I don't need to type it in every time I open Workstation and access this VM.

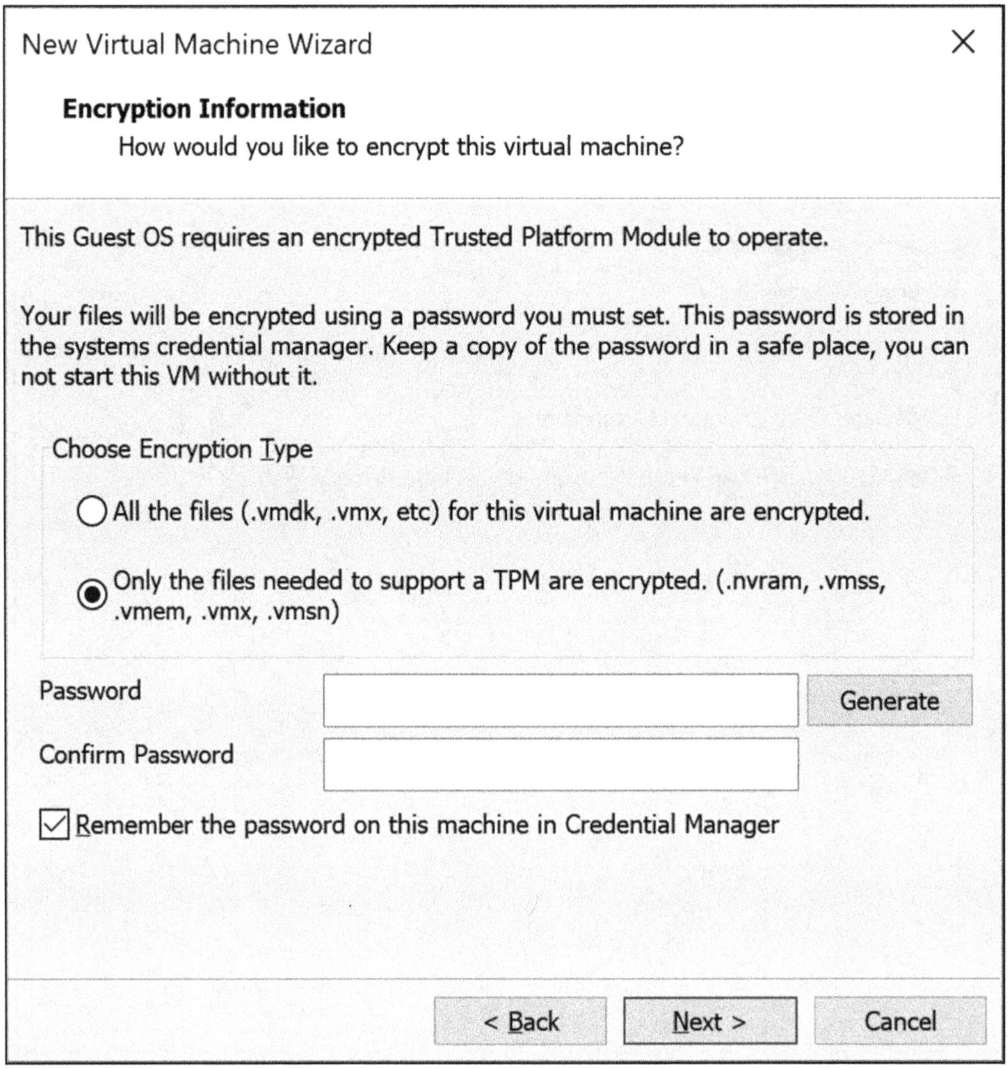

New Virtual Machine Wizard   ✕

Encryption Information
How would you like to encrypt this virtual machine?

This Guest OS requires an encrypted Trusted Platform Module to operate.

Your files will be encrypted using a password you must set. This password is stored in the systems credential manager. Keep a copy of the password in a safe place, you can not start this VM without it.

Choose Encryption Type

○ All the files (.vmdk, .vmx, etc) for this virtual machine are encrypted.

◉ Only the files needed to support a TPM are encrypted. (.nvram, .vmss, .vmem, .vmx, .vmsn)

Password [   ] [Generate]

Confirm Password [   ]

☑ Remember the password on this machine in Credential Manager

[< Back] [Next >] [Cancel]

Figure 4.11

Next, I will be asked to specify how large I want the disk on the VM to be. It will give me a suggested size based on the OS of 60GB so I will stick with that. You can increase this if you need more space, assuming you have the room on your host's hard drive.

Next, I will have an option to store the virtual disk as a single file or to split it into multiple files. If you plan on backing up your virtual machines, then multiple files might be the better option. I never do and like to have one file for my virtual disk because it makes things easier to manage, especially if I want to attach the virtual disk to a different VM.

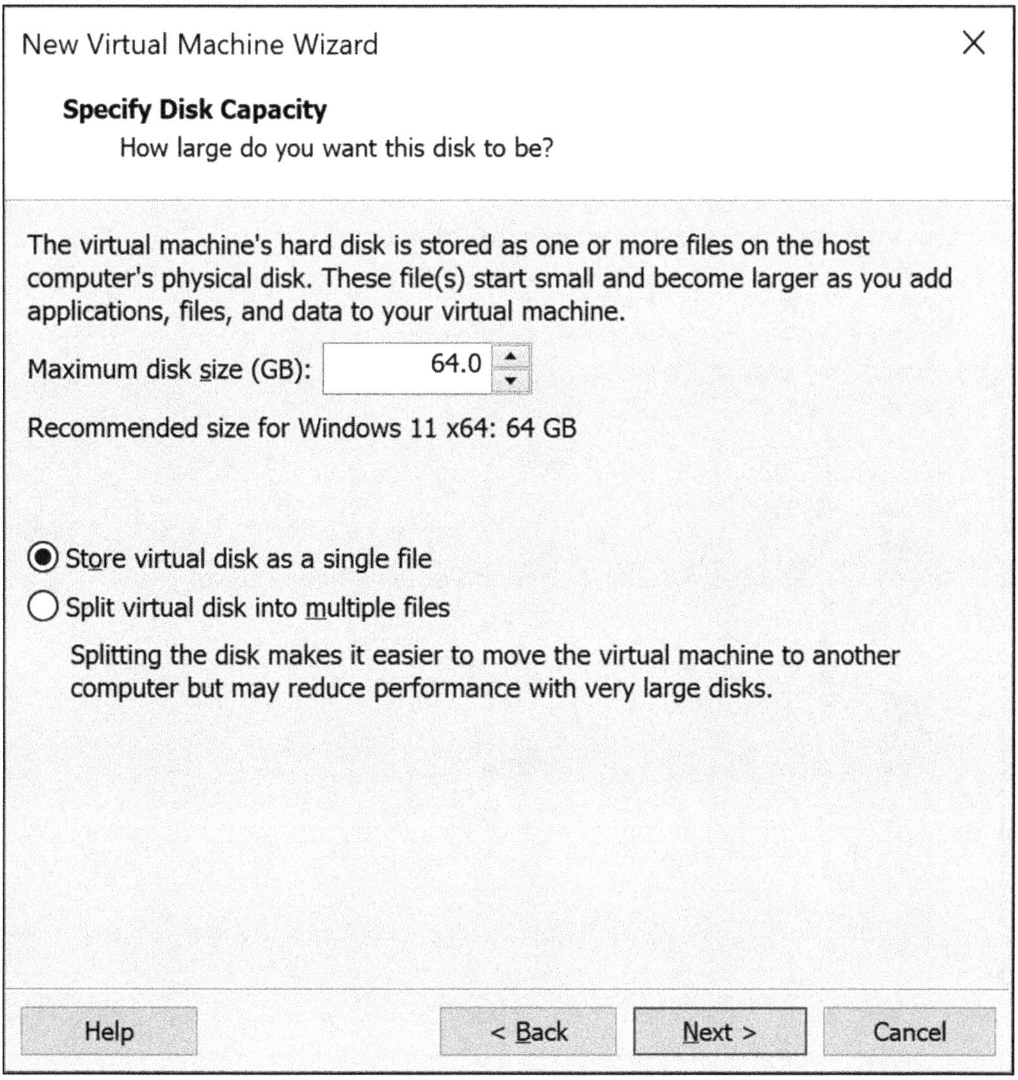

New Virtual Machine Wizard   ✕

Specify Disk Capacity
    How large do you want this disk to be?

The virtual machine's hard disk is stored as one or more files on the host
computer's physical disk. These file(s) start small and become larger as you add
applications, files, and data to your virtual machine.

Maximum disk size (GB):   64.0 ▲
                                       ▼

Recommended size for Windows 11 x64: 64 GB

◉ Store virtual disk as a single file
◯ Split virtual disk into multiple files

    Splitting the disk makes it easier to move the virtual machine to another
    computer but may reduce performance with very large disks.

         Help   < Back   Next >   Cancel

Figure 4.12

Now I will be shown a summary of your virtual machine's configuration. If you
want to make changes, you can click on the *Customize Hardware* button to do so.

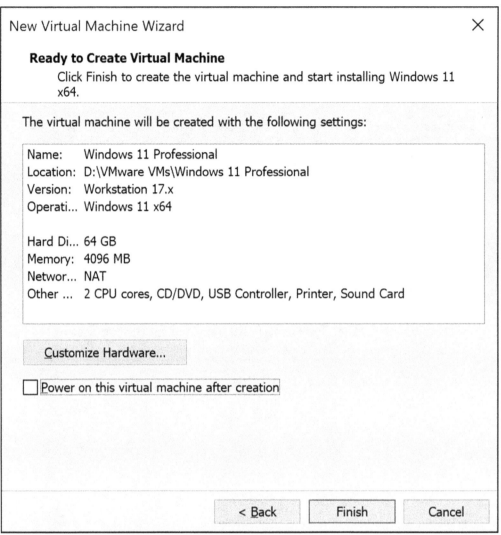

Figure 4.13

Once I click the *Finish* button, I will see my new VM listed in my inventory, and it will not be running. From here I can edit the VM and make changes or start it up to begin the operating system installation from my ISO file.

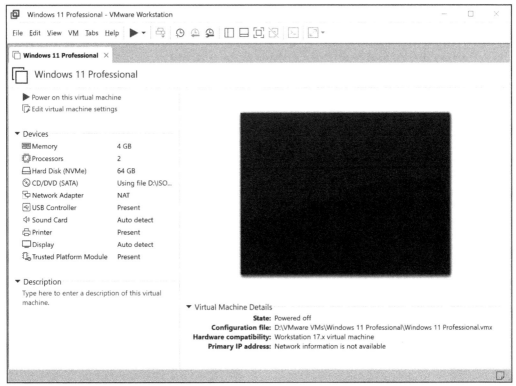

Figure 4.14

For the next virtual machine I will be creating, I will use the Custom method to show you the difference. You will notice that many of the screens are the same as the Typical method but there are many additional options you can configure as you go along.

On the first screen, you will see that you can choose a different hardware compatibility level if you need to. It will default to the version that matches your VMware Workstation installation. You might need to run an older version for compatibility with other hypervisors or the operating system you plan to run on the VM.

45

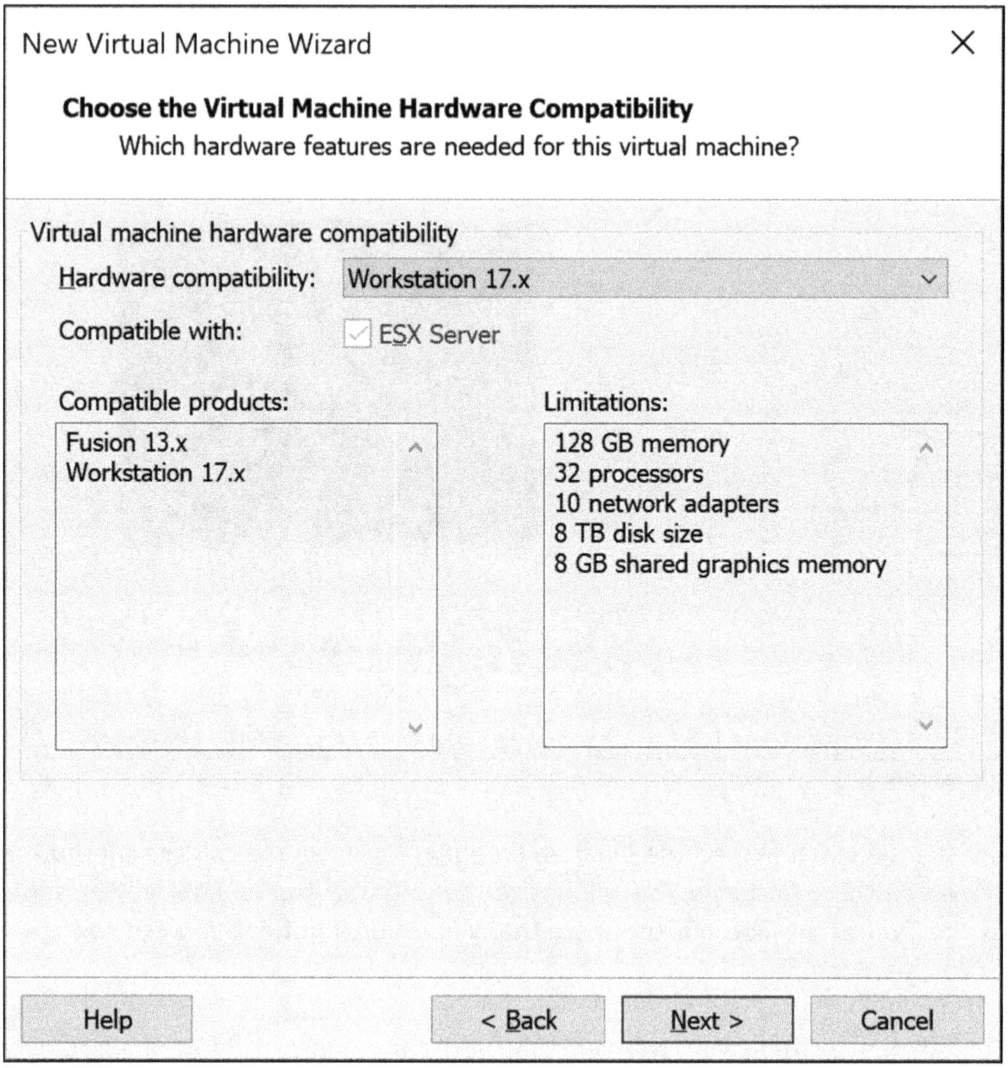

New Virtual Machine Wizard   ✕

Choose the Virtual Machine Hardware Compatibility
Which hardware features are needed for this virtual machine?

Virtual machine hardware compatibility

Hardware compatibility: Workstation 17.x   ⌄

Compatible with: ☑ ESX Server

Compatible products:

Fusion 13.x
Workstation 17.x

Limitations:

128 GB memory
32 processors
10 network adapters
8 TB disk size
8 GB shared graphics memory

Help   < Back   Next >   Cancel

Figure 4.15

Next, you will have the same guest operating screen as you did for the Typical method. I will once again choose my Windows 11 ISO file.

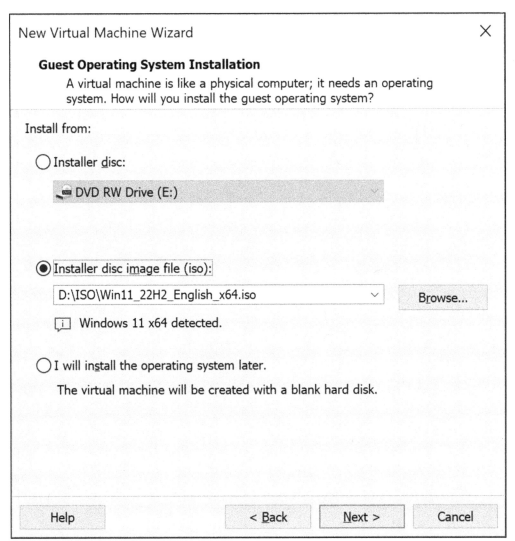

Figure 4.16

The next two screens will also be the same as we saw with the Typical method. The Select Guest Operating System will only be shown if Workstation does not recognize the OS type from ISO file or CD.

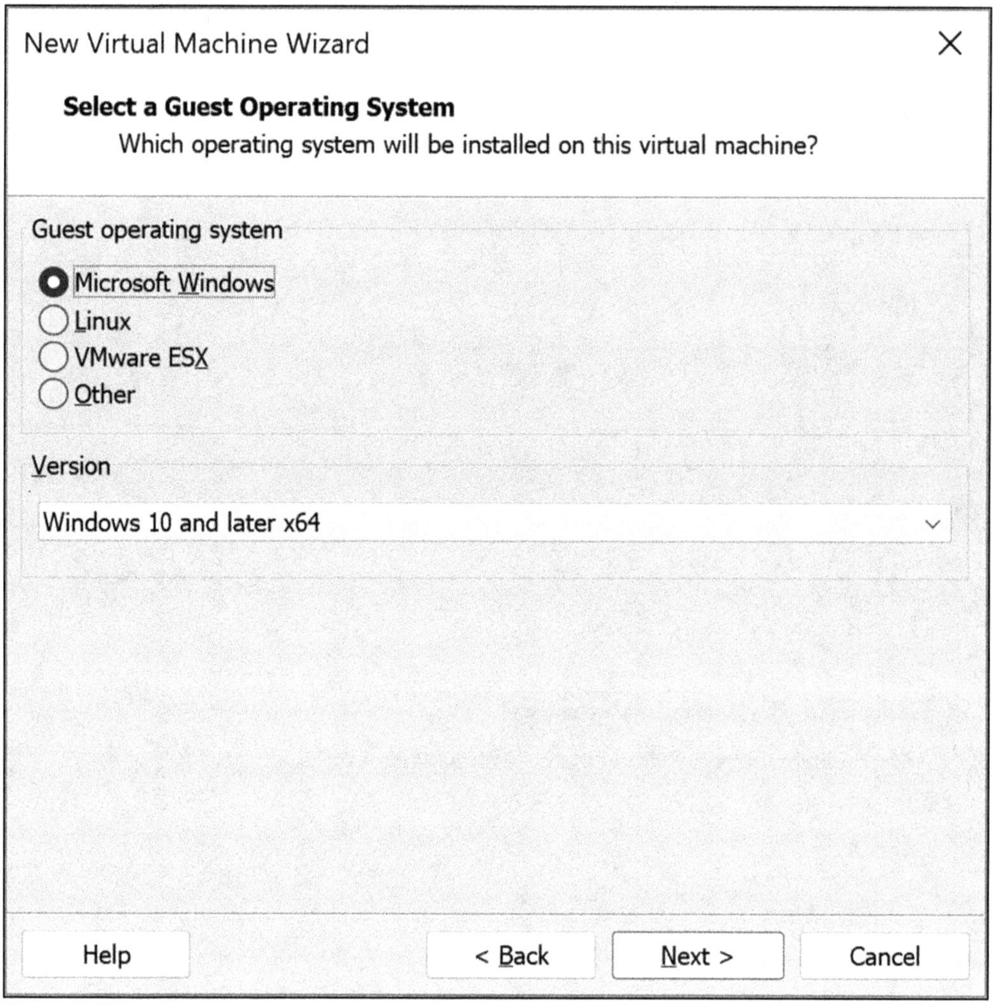

New Virtual Machine Wizard   ✕

Select a Guest Operating System
Which operating system will be installed on this virtual machine?

Guest operating system

● Microsoft Windows
○ Linux
○ VMware ESX
○ Other

Version

Windows 10 and later x64   ⌄

| Help | | < Back | Next > | Cancel |

Figure 4.17

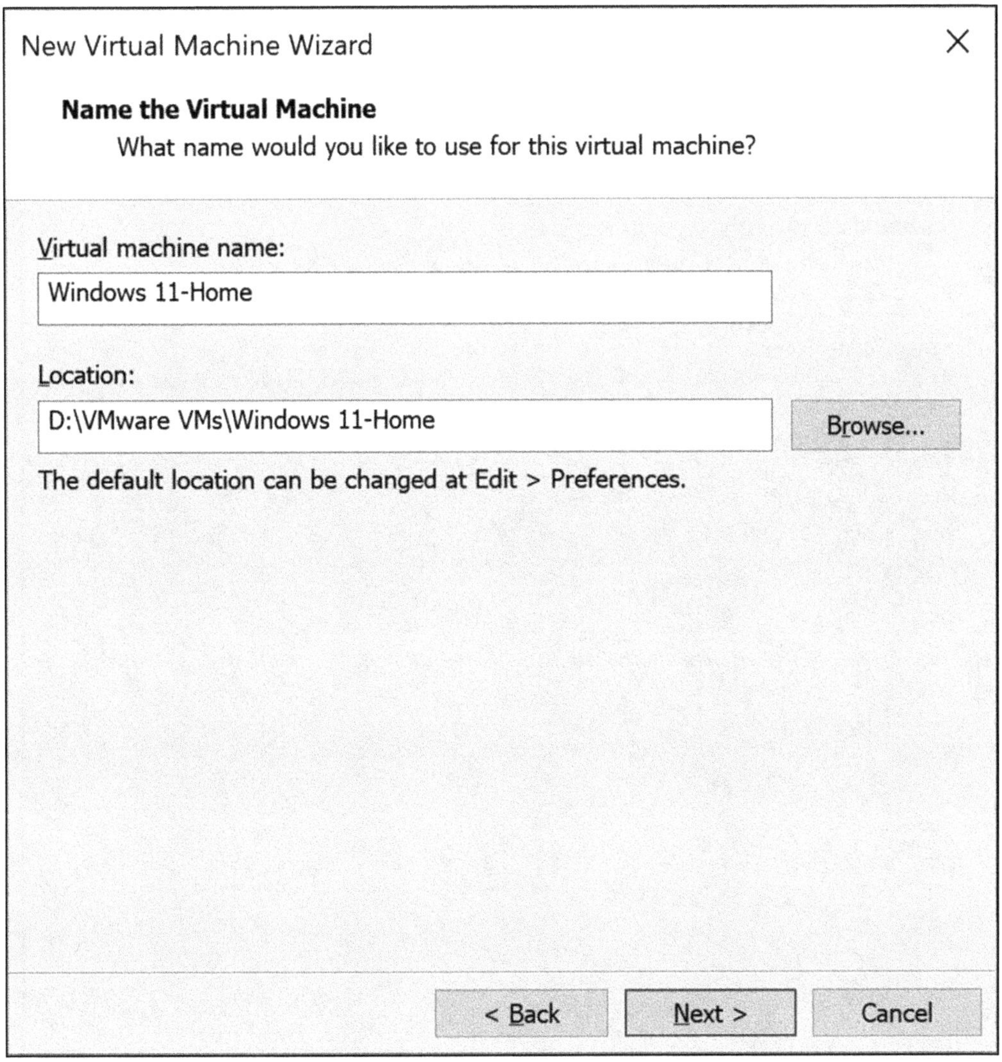

New Virtual Machine Wizard   ✕

Name the Virtual Machine

What name would you like to use for this virtual machine?

Virtual machine name:

Windows 11-Home

Location:

D:\VMware VMs\Windows 11-Home   Browse...

The default location can be changed at Edit > Preferences.

    < Back   Next >   Cancel

Figure 4.18

If you are installing Windows 11 again, you will need to type in the encryption password like you did using the typical method.

On the next screen, you can choose whether your virtual machine will use a BIOS for its firmware boot device or the newer UEFI. Unless you have a specific reason to use a BIOS, you should choose UEFI.

The *Secure Boot* option is used to help ensure that your VM boots using only software that is trusted by the PC manufacturer. You will most likely not need to use this unless you are using the VM for something that requires that type of security or if you are really trying to prevent malware from loading up with your computer.

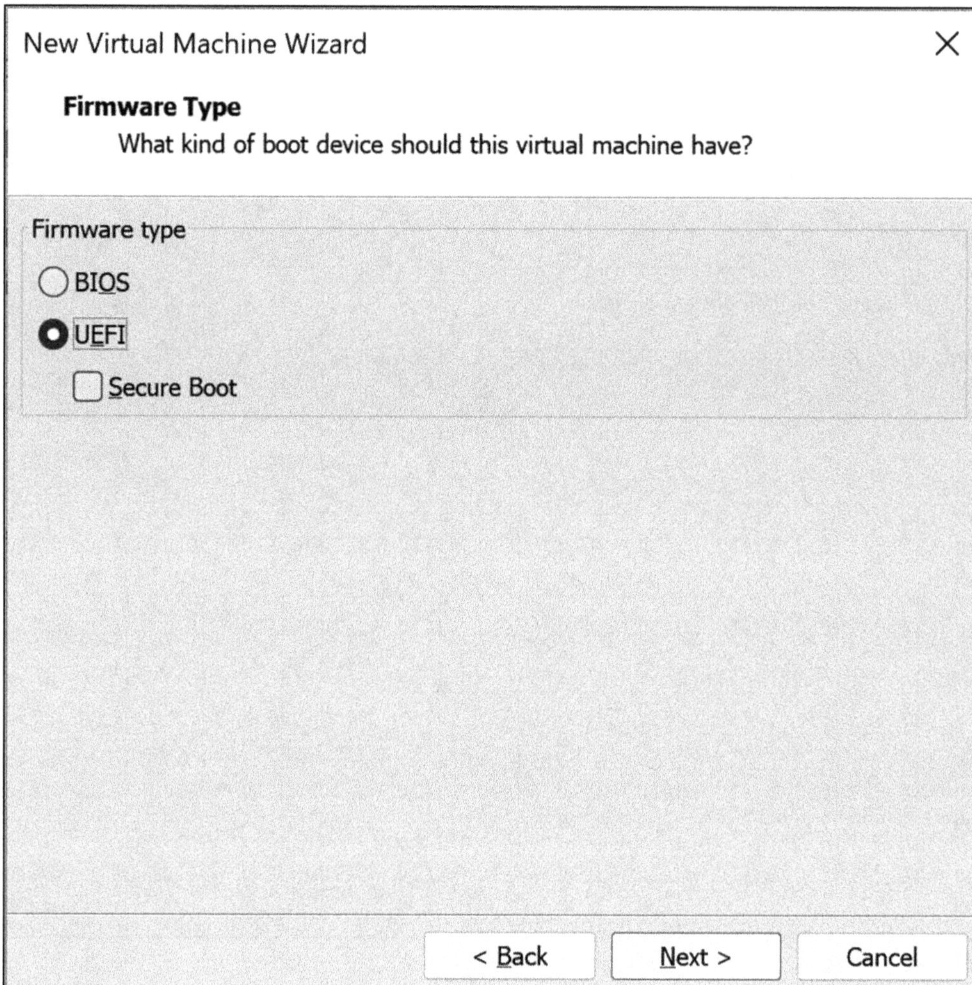

New Virtual Machine Wizard   ×

Firmware Type
What kind of boot device should this virtual machine have?

Firmware type

○ BIOS

● UEFI

☐ Secure Boot

< Back   Next >   Cancel

Figure 4.19

Next, you will be able to specify how many processors you want to use for your VM and how many cores each processor will have. For a typical VM that will be performing basic tasks, 1 processor and 2 cores should be fine. For a server, you might want to go with 2 processors with 2 or 4 cores each. You should look at the recommended hardware requirements for any applications you are running on your virtual machine. Just because you can assign 16 processors with 8 cores each, doesn't mean you should do it!

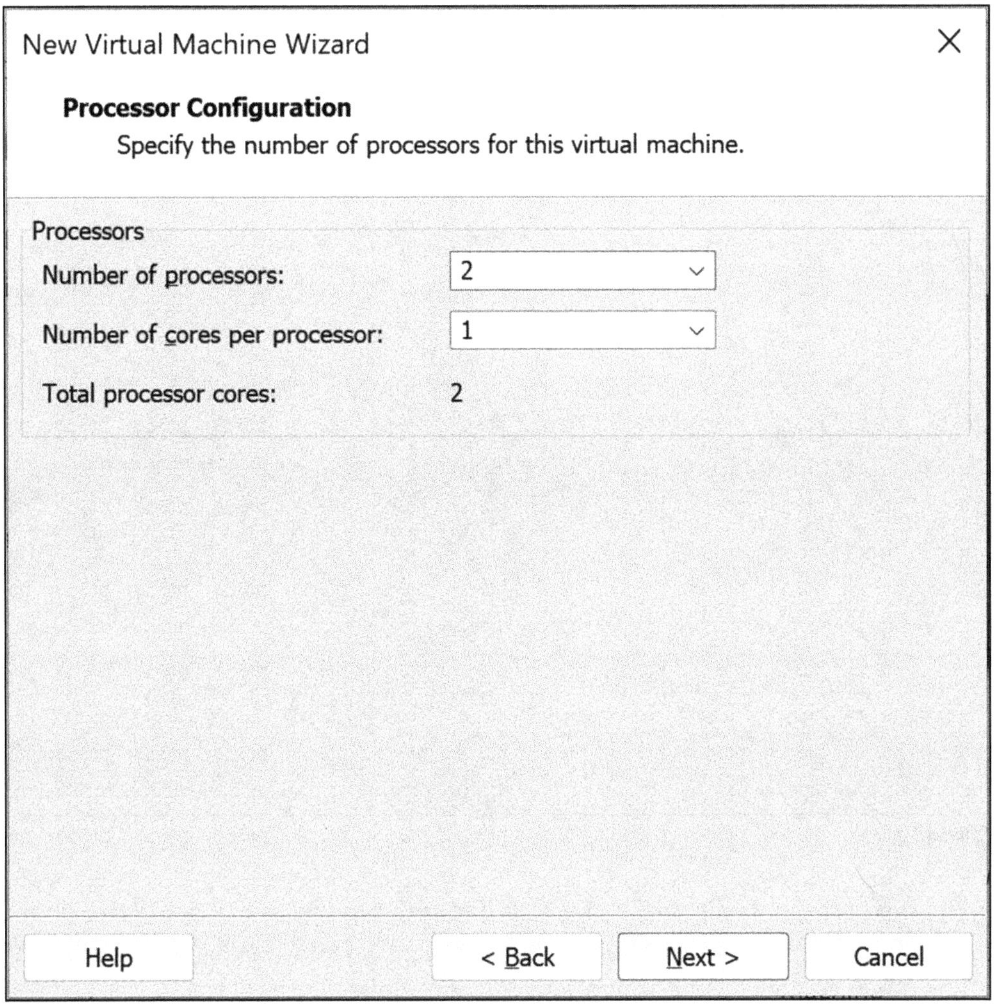

New Virtual Machine Wizard   ✕

Processor Configuration
    Specify the number of processors for this virtual machine.

Processors

Number of processors: | 2   ⌄ |

Number of cores per processor: | 1   ⌄ |

Total processor cores: 2

| Help | | < Back | | Next > | | Cancel |

Figure 4.20

Next, I will be shown the Customize Hardware screen automatically and once again, I will bump up the RAM to 8GB and leave the rest as is.

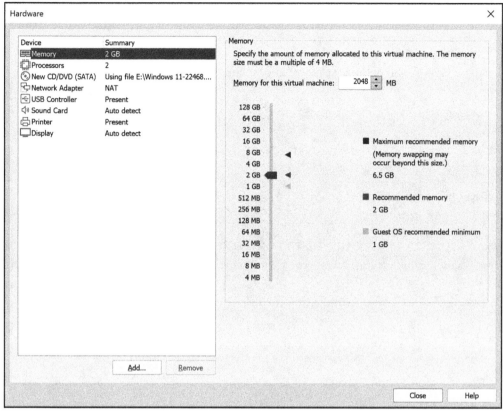

Figure 4.21

On the next screen, I will be asked which network type I want to configure on my virtual machine. If this VM needs internet access, then leave the default NAT setting. I will be going over networking in more detail in chapter 6.

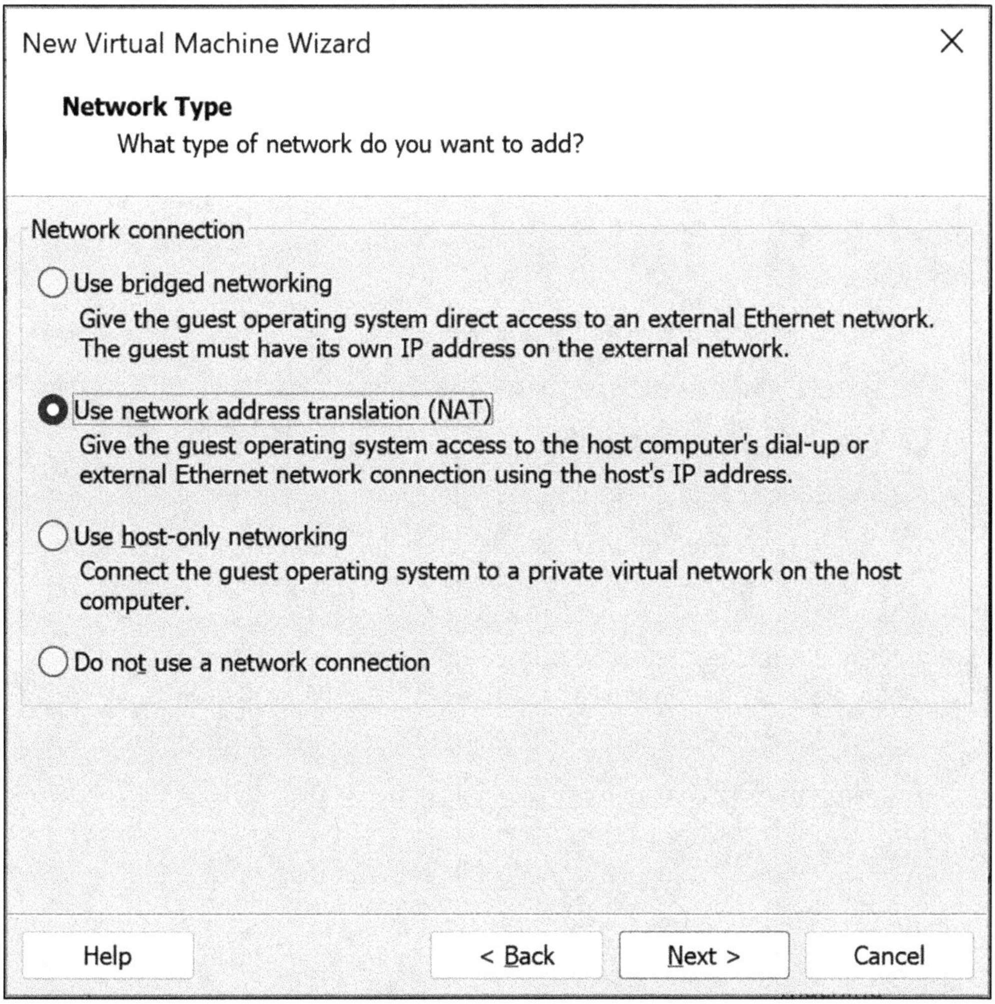

New Virtual Machine Wizard   ✕

Network Type
    What type of network do you want to add?

Network connection

○ Use bridged networking
    Give the guest operating system direct access to an external Ethernet network.
    The guest must have its own IP address on the external network.

● Use network address translation (NAT)
    Give the guest operating system access to the host computer's dial-up or
    external Ethernet network connection using the host's IP address.

○ Use host-only networking
    Connect the guest operating system to a private virtual network on the host
    computer.

○ Do not use a network connection

Help		< Back	Next >	Cancel

Figure 4.22

If you need a specific SCSI controller type, you can choose it here assuming the choices available are what you are looking for. If it's just a typical VM then stick with the LSI Logic SAS option. Paravirtualized SCSI is used for high performance storage adapters that can provide greater throughput with lower CPU utilization.

New Virtual Machine Wizard ✕

Select I/O Controller Types
Which SCSI controller type would you like to use for SCSI virtual disks?

I/O controller types

SCSI Controller:

○ BusLogic   (Not available for 64-bit guests)

○ LSI Logic   (Not supported by Windows 10 and later x64)

● LSI Logic SAS   (Recommended)

○ Paravirtualized SCSI

| Help | | < Back | Next > | Cancel |

Figure 4.23

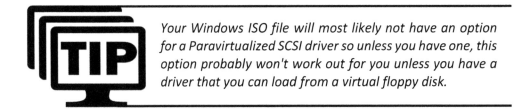

Your Windows ISO file will most likely not have an option for a Paravirtualized SCSI driver so unless you have one, this option probably won't work out for you unless you have a driver that you can load from a virtual floppy disk.

Next, I will be asked to choose my virtual hard disk type. The default option will be NVMe, but you can choose one of the older technologies if you need it for a specific operating system. You can think of NVMe as solid state (SSD) disks for your virtual machines.

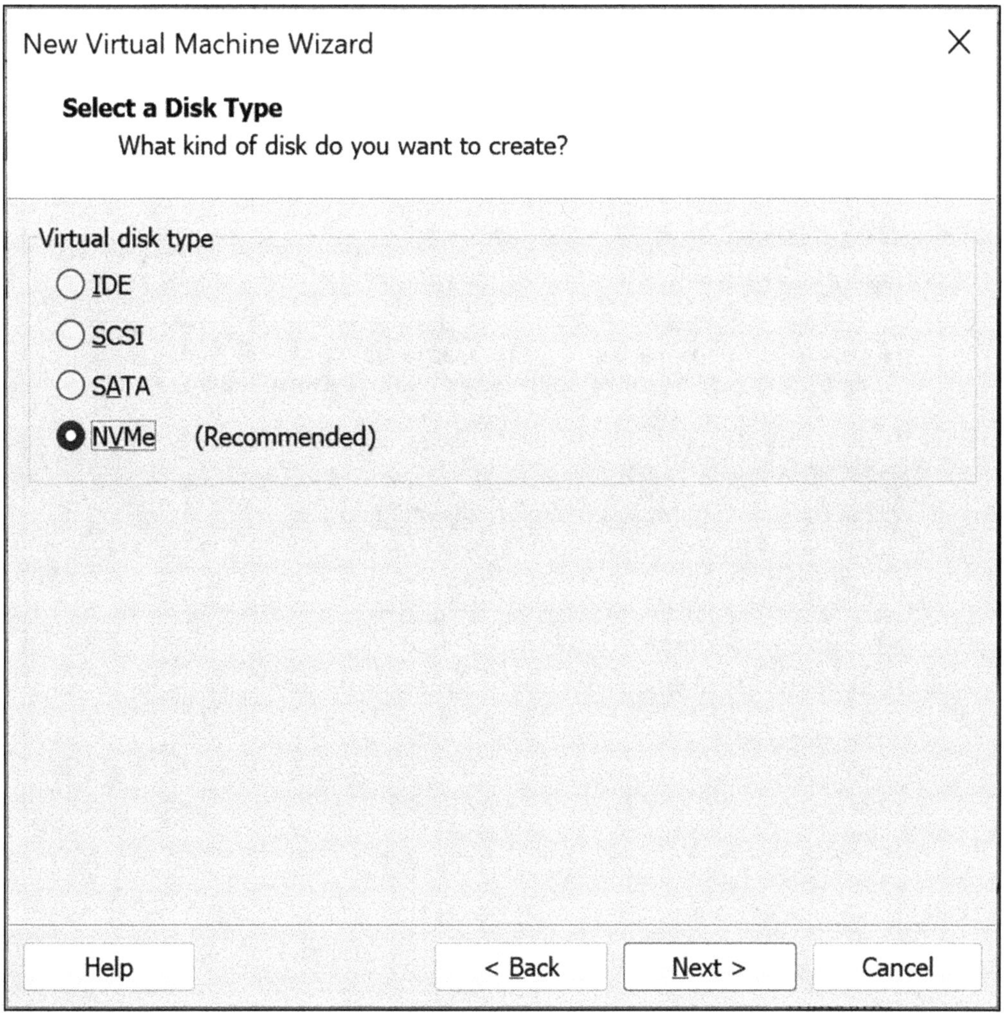

New Virtual Machine Wizard   ✕

Select a Disk Type
What kind of disk do you want to create?

Virtual disk type
◯ IDE
◯ SCSI
◯ SATA
◉ NVMe   (Recommended)

Help   < Back   Next >   Cancel

Figure 4.24

The Custom method will allow me to create a new virtual disk or attach and existing virtual disk that I had from another virtual machine, assuming it has been detached from that VM first. You can also use the physical disk option to give direct access to a hard drive on your host.

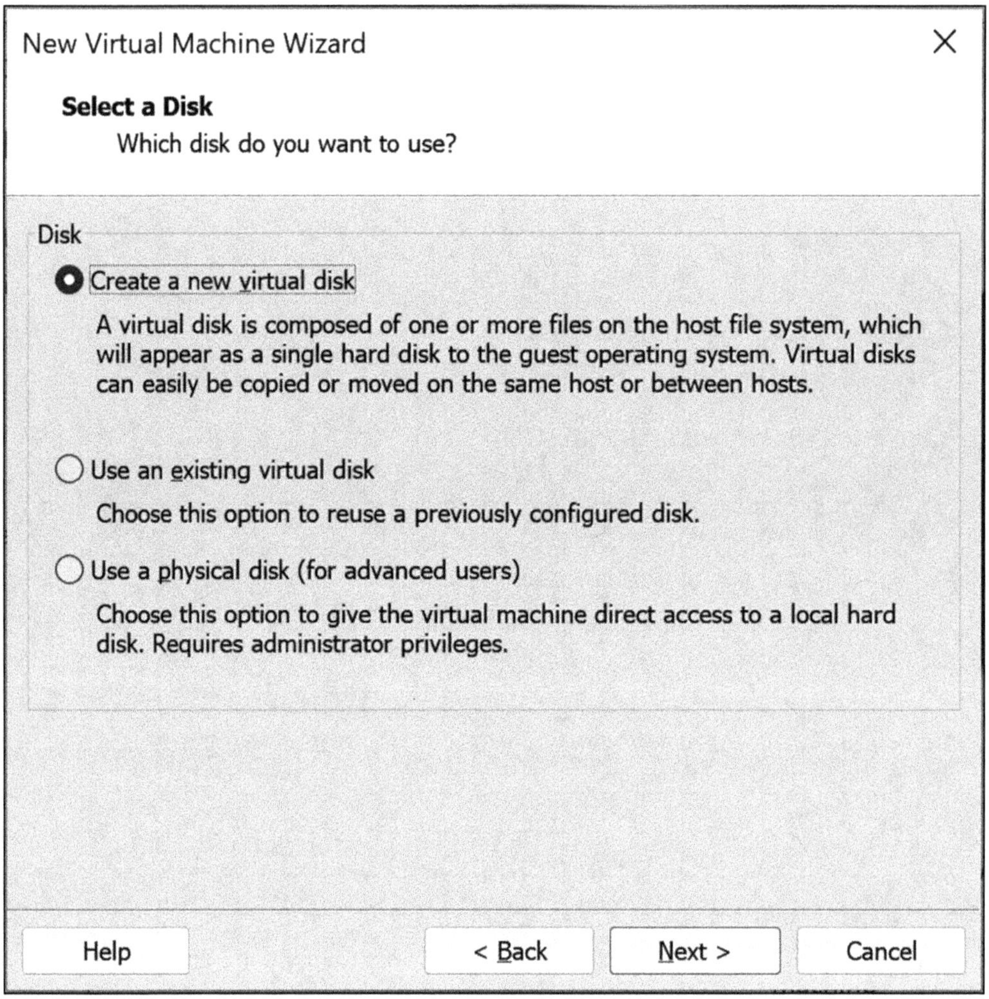

New Virtual Machine Wizard   ✕

Select a Disk
    Which disk do you want to use?

Disk
    ⦿ Create a new virtual disk

    A virtual disk is composed of one or more files on the host file system, which
    will appear as a single hard disk to the guest operating system. Virtual disks
    can easily be copied or moved on the same host or between hosts.

    ◯ Use an existing virtual disk

    Choose this option to reuse a previously configured disk.

    ◯ Use a physical disk (for advanced users)

    Choose this option to give the virtual machine direct access to a local hard
    disk. Requires administrator privileges.

    Help   < Back   Next >   Cancel

Figure 4.25

The disk capacity options are a little different for the Custom method because
you can choose to allocate all the disk space immediately or have it grow as
needed until it gets to the specified disk size. This is known as a dynamic disk
because it will only use the space it needs on your host hard drive as it grows. So
if you allocate your VM 60GB for the hard drive and the VM is only using 20GB of
that space, you will only be out 20GB of space on the host's hard drive. I always
like to check this option because it helps reduce storage space on the host and
there is a minimal performance hit when doing so… if any.

For this virtual machine, I will be choosing the option to split the virtual disk files
into multiple files so you can see what happens when you do so.

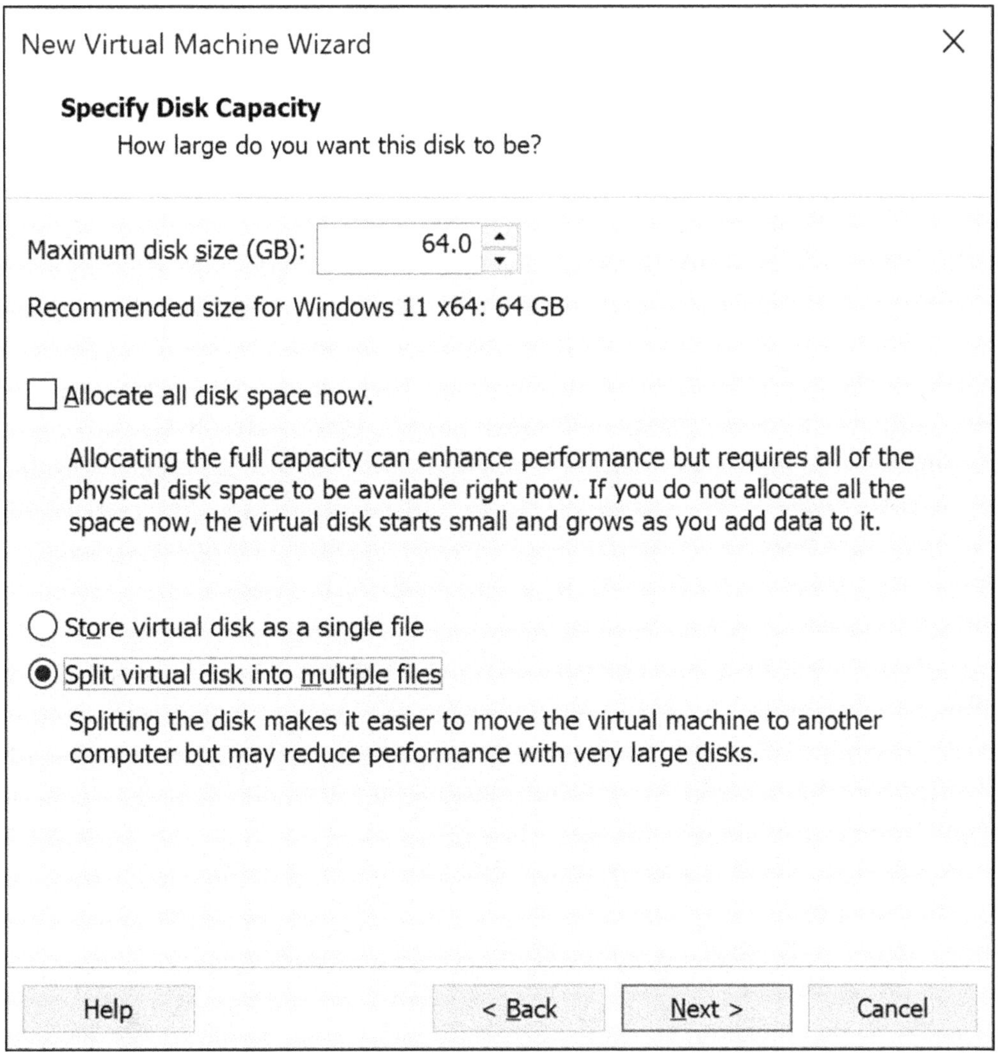

New Virtual Machine Wizard   ✕

Specify Disk Capacity
> How large do you want this disk to be?

Maximum disk size (GB):   64.0 ▲▼

Recommended size for Windows 11 x64: 64 GB

☐ Allocate all disk space now.

> Allocating the full capacity can enhance performance but requires all of the physical disk space to be available right now. If you do not allocate all the space now, the virtual disk starts small and grows as you add data to it.

○ Store virtual disk as a single file
◉ Split virtual disk into multiple files

> Splitting the disk makes it easier to move the virtual machine to another computer but may reduce performance with very large disks.

Help		< Back	Next >	Cancel

Figure 4.26

The Custom method will also let you name your virtual disk file and give you the option to store it in a different location from the other virtual machine files if needed.

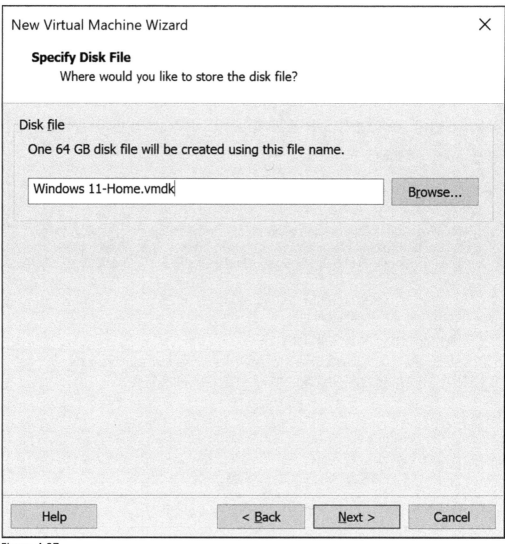

Figure 4.27

Finally, you will get the same summary screen where you can customize the hardware again before finalizing the VM creation process.

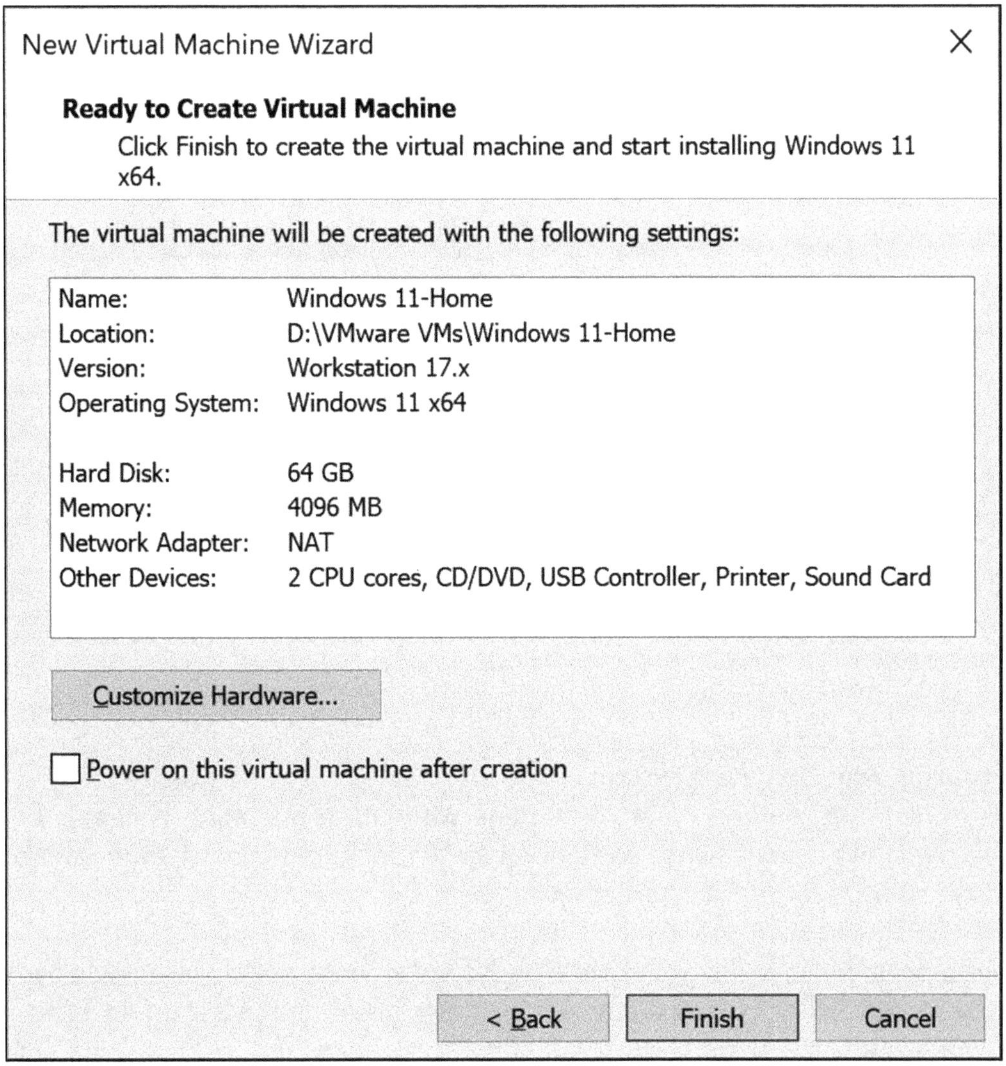

New Virtual Machine Wizard   ✕

Ready to Create Virtual Machine
Click Finish to create the virtual machine and start installing Windows 11 x64.

The virtual machine will be created with the following settings:

Name:	Windows 11-Home
Location:	D:\VMware VMs\Windows 11-Home
Version:	Workstation 17.x
Operating System:	Windows 11 x64
Hard Disk:	64 GB
Memory:	4096 MB
Network Adapter:	NAT
Other Devices:	2 CPU cores, CD/DVD, USB Controller, Printer, Sound Card

Customize Hardware...

☐ Power on this virtual machine after creation

< Back   Finish   Cancel

Figure 4.28

Figure 4.29 shows my new VM with its multiple disk files (.vmdk) and you can see why it's easier to manage when you only have one!

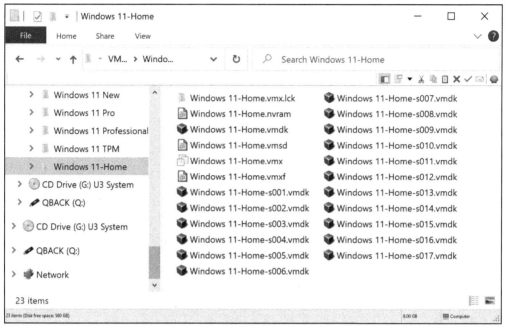

Figure 4.29

Installing Your Operating System

As I mentioned before, a virtual machine without an operating system is not much good to anyone. Once you get your VM configured you will then want to install your OS so you can start using it.

The process for installing your operating system will vary depending on what you choose to install. Microsoft Windows is pretty to install and so is Linux if you have some experience with it. You will find that once you start getting into virtualization you will be installing operating systems on a regular basis and will be able to do it with your eyes closed.

For my example, I will be installing Windows 11 on my new VM. I will not go through the entire process because it's pretty straightforward and also because Microsoft changes the steps on a semi regular basis so it's never quite the same.

*If you want to learn more about Windows 11 and improve your Windows skills, then check out my book titled **Windows 11 Made Easy**.*
https://www.amazon.com/dp/B09HFXWXRY

To begin the process, I will need to make sure that my Windows ISO file is still mounted in my virtual DVD drive which it should be if you didn't remove it or remove the ISO file from its original location.

Next, I will click the green play button to power on the virtual machine and want for the typical *press any key to boot from CD* message and then press a key on my keyboard.

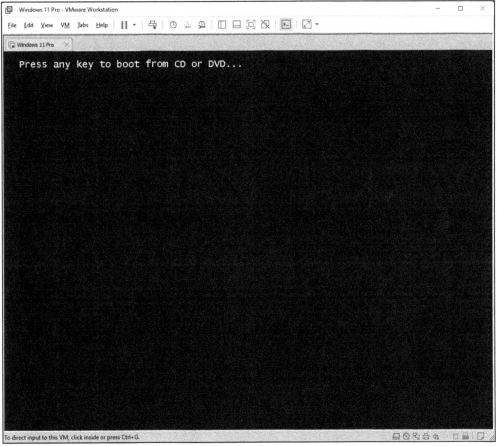

Figure 4.30

Make sure you click your mouse inside the console window so that your keyboard and mouse are active in the VM otherwise you might miss your chance to press any key to boot from CD and have to reset the VM and try again.

Next, I will get the first Windows installation screen where I can choose my language and begin the installation process. Take a look at the bottom of figure 4.31 and you will see a message asking me to install VMware Tools on my new VM. Obviously, I can't install them until Windows is fully installed first so I usually just click on *Remind me later* and install them when I have Windows installed.

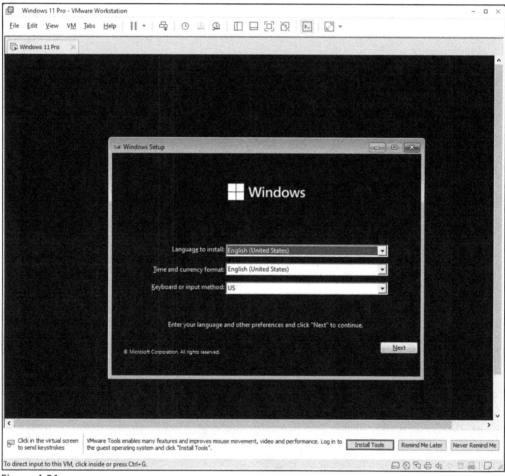

Figure 4.31

Installing VMware Tools

Once you have your operating system installed, you should install the VMware Tools software to enhance the performance of your virtual machine. VMware tools will make the virtual machine run smoother, allow for higher resolution and color depth, give your VM sound, allow you to drag and drop files between your host and guest and also copy and paste text etc.

To install VMware Tools, make sure the VM is running and logged in and go to the VM menu and choose *Install VMware Tools*. Then you will say Yes to the UAC prompt to continue.

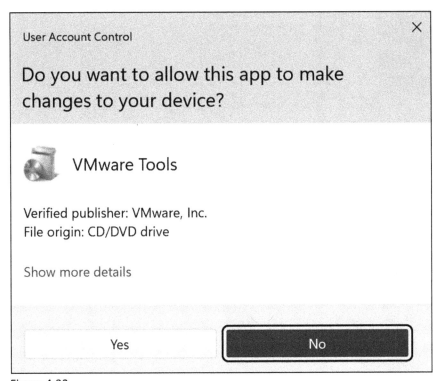

Figure 4.32

After that, it's a typical Windows software installation like you have probably seen 100 times before where you click next until you are done.

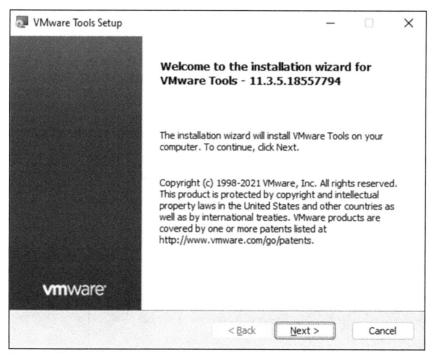

Figure 4.33

I always choose the *Typical* option when installing the tools on a virtual machine.

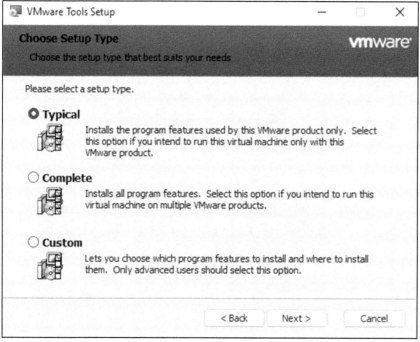

Figure 4.34

After the tools have finished installing, you will be prompted to reboot the computer so all of the enhancements can take effect.

Deleting a Virtual Machine

One of the best things about virtualization is that it makes it easy to create virtual machines for testing and if you mess something up, you can just start over again and have a new VM up and running in minutes.

I like to use virtual machines for software testing before installing the new software on my main computer to see how it works and to see how it affects other programs on my machine. That way, if something goes horribly wrong, I don't risk hurting my main PC and can simply get rid of the VM and start again. Of course I can always take a snapshot of the virtual machine before installing the software and then revert back to it if needed. I will be discussing snapshots in chapter 7.

If you do need to delete a virtual machine for any reason, it's a very simple process. If you right click on a VM in your library and choose Remove, it will remove it from the library itself but will not delete it from your computer.

If you want to permanently delete a virtual machine, you can select that VM, go to the *VM* menu, click on *Manage* and then choose *Delete from Disk*. You will then get a warning message telling you that your virtual machine will be deleted for good. You should look at the message to make sure the path is pointing to the correct VM and that you didn't accidentally select one that you didn't want to delete.

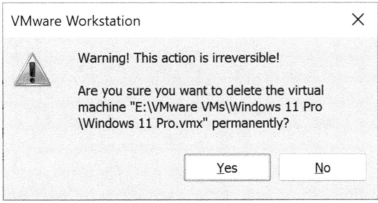

Figure 4.35

Once you click the *Yes* button, the virtual machine will be removed from the VMware Workstation inventory and also your hard drive.

Technically you can also go to the folder on your host computer that contains the virtual machine files and delete it that way. Then when you go back into Workstation it will tell you that it can't find the VM and ask if you want it removed from the inventory.

Chapter 5 - Virtual Machine Settings

Once you have created a virtual machine, that doesn't necessarily mean you are done and will not need to make any changes to it. You will most likely find yourself needing to adjust settings and make changes to the hardware to do things such as increase performance or add more hard disk space.

Having the ability to make adjustments as needed is one of the great things about virtualization. For example, if you needed more RAM in a physical server, you would have to find the right type, shut down the computer, install the RAM and then reboot it. For a VMware Workstation VM, you can simply go to the settings and increase the amount of RAM without even shutting down the VM (in most cases).

Hardware Settings

Adding, removing and editing hardware for a virtual machine is a fairly easy process and it can all be done from one place. To get to the VM hardware settings, select the virtual machine you want to adjust and then go to the *VM* menu and choose *Settings*. You can also right click the tab for the VM and choose Settings from there.

Figure 5.1 shows the settings screen for one of my virtual machines for the RAM settings. As you can see, the list on the left tells me what hardware is configured for this VM. As you click on a specific hardware device, the settings on the right will change accordingly.

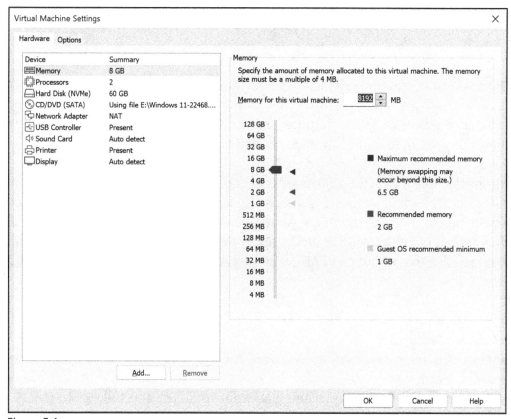

Figure 5.1

Figure 5.2 shows how the hardware settings change when I click on the *Display* device. Certain hardware devices will have many more configurable settings than others.

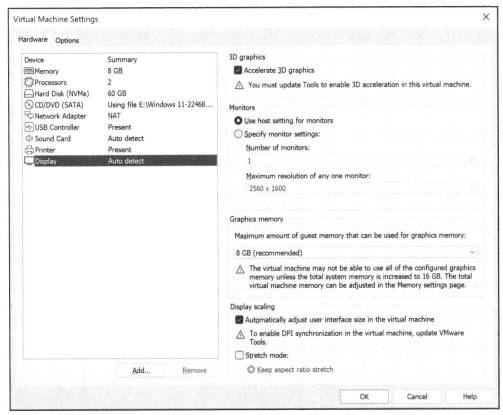

Figure 5.2

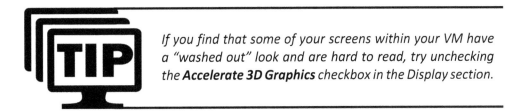

*If you find that some of your screens within your VM have a "washed out" look and are hard to read, try unchecking the **Accelerate 3D Graphics** checkbox in the Display section.*

Adding & Editing Hardware

Like I mentioned previously, editing your hardware settings is a pretty easy process but one thing you need to keep in mind is that some of these settings can only be done when the virtual machine is powered off. If you run into a situation like this, you will be told that you need to shut down the VM before being able to change the setting.

Now let's say I want to increase the size of our main hard drive and then add a secondary hard drive to the VM. To increase the size of the existing disk, I will go to the Hard Disk section to begin the process. As you can see in figure 5.3, I am shown the details about my hard drive such as its location, capacity and other information. You can see that the current size is only 7.6 MB and that is because I haven't installed an operating system on this VM yet. It also shows that the maximum size is 60GB. This tells me that this VM was configured with a dynamic disk that expands as needed up to 60GB. Under the *Disk information* section it also says that *Disk space is not preallocated for this hard disk* which confirms that it's a dynamic disk.

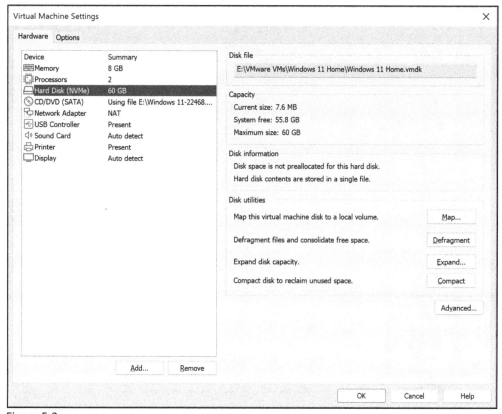

Figure 5.3

To increase the size of the hard disk, I will click on the *Expand* button. I will be asked to enter the new size of the disk. It was originally 60GB so I will change it to 80GB and click the Expand button.

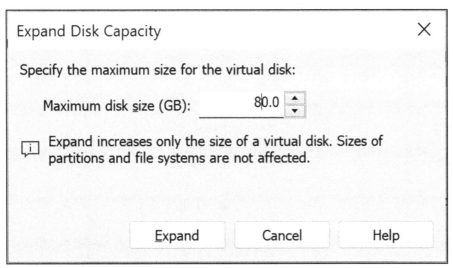

Figure 5.4

After the process is complete, I would need to go into the operating system on the VM and increase the disk size there. For example, I would use Disk Management in Windows to apply the new space to my disk volume.

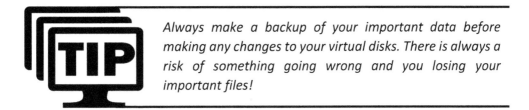

Always make a backup of your important data before making any changes to your virtual disks. There is always a risk of something going wrong and you losing your important files!

For my next example, I will add an additional virtual hard disk to the VM by clicking on the *Add* button at the bottom of the screen (figure 5.3). I will then be asked what type of hardware I wish to add. I will select *Hard Disk* and click the *Next* button.

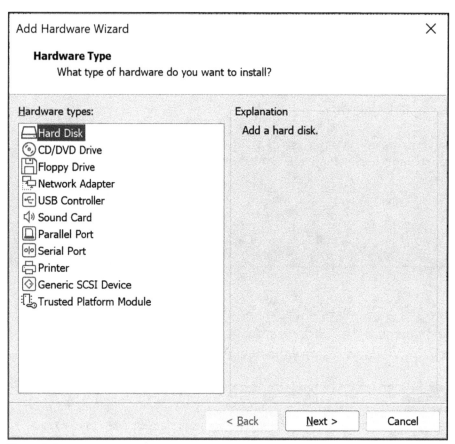

Figure 5.5

I will then go with the recommended hard disk type (NVMe) and click Next.

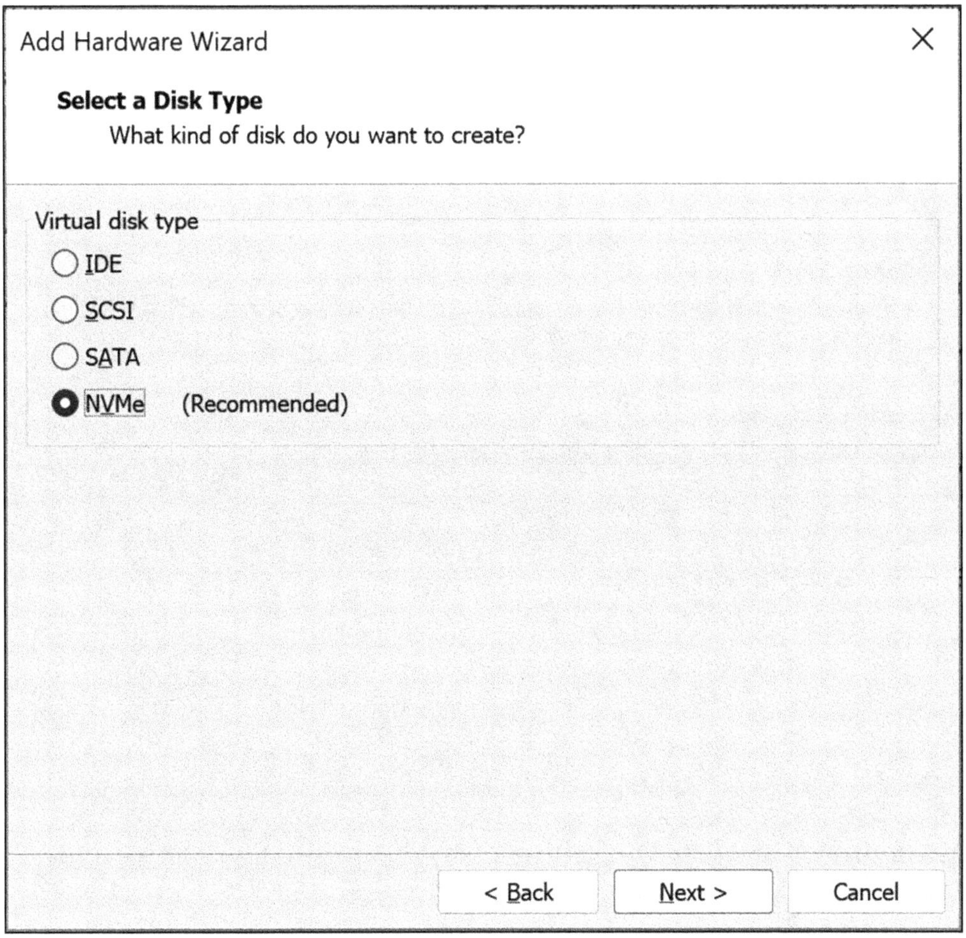

Add Hardware Wizard ✕

Select a Disk Type
What kind of disk do you want to create?

Virtual disk type

◯ IDE

◯ SCSI

◯ SATA

🔘 NVMe   (Recommended)

< Back   Next >   Cancel

Figure 5.6

I will then choose the *Create a new disk option* and click Next again. You are probably thinking that this process looks familiar. That's because it was the same process we did when creating a virtual machine and adding the hard drive.

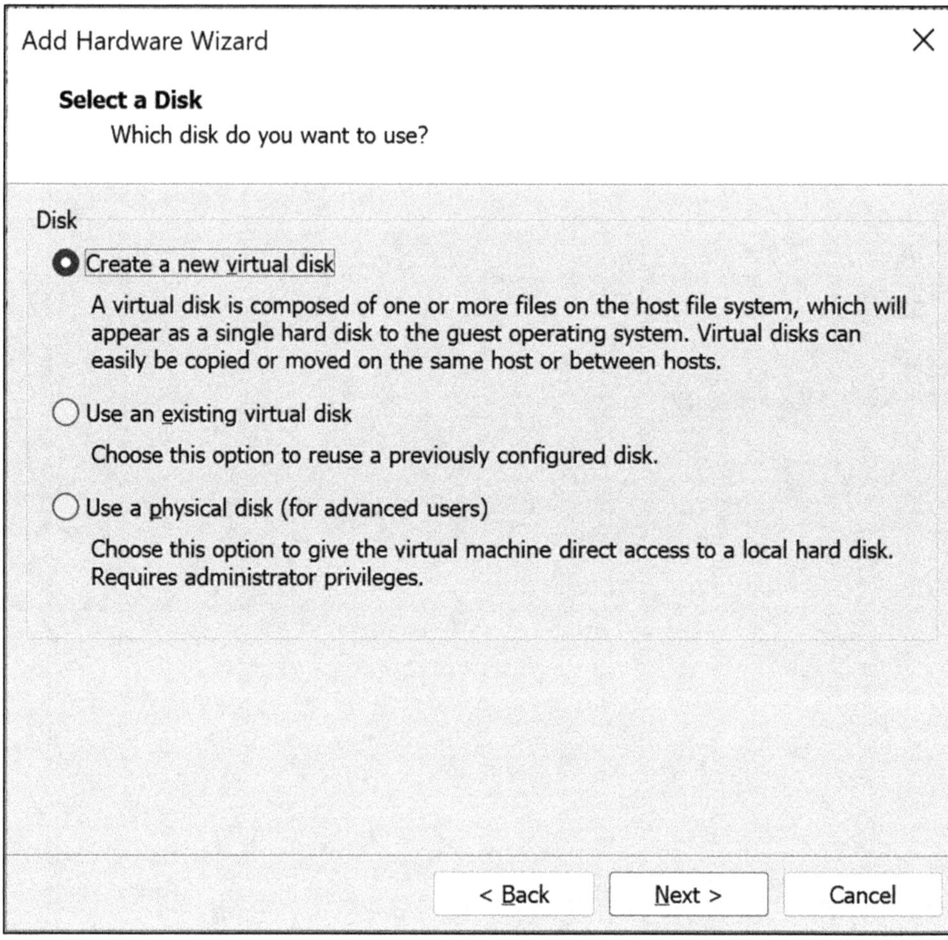

Add Hardware Wizard   ✕

Select a Disk
        Which disk do you want to use?

Disk

   ● Create a new virtual disk

     A virtual disk is composed of one or more files on the host file system, which will
     appear as a single hard disk to the guest operating system. Virtual disks can
     easily be copied or moved on the same host or between hosts.

   ○ Use an existing virtual disk

     Choose this option to reuse a previously configured disk.

   ○ Use a physical disk (for advanced users)

     Choose this option to give the virtual machine direct access to a local hard disk.
     Requires administrator privileges.

                              < Back   Next >   Cancel

Figure 5.7

I will make this new disk 40GB and have it stored as a single disk file.

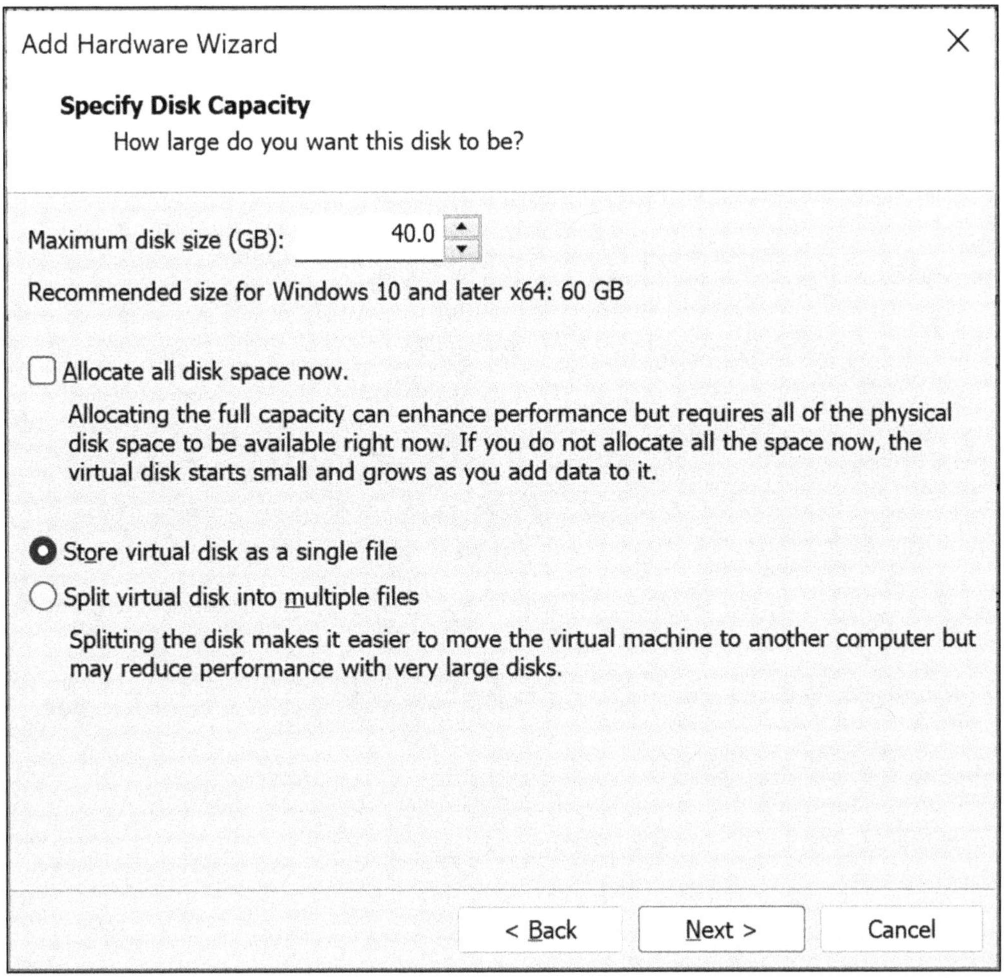

Add Hardware Wizard   ✕

Specify Disk Capacity
        How large do you want this disk to be?

Maximum disk size (GB):   40.0 ▲▼

Recommended size for Windows 10 and later x64: 60 GB

☐ Allocate all disk space now.

   Allocating the full capacity can enhance performance but requires all of the physical
   disk space to be available right now. If you do not allocate all the space now, the
   virtual disk starts small and grows as you add data to it.

◉ Store virtual disk as a single file

○ Split virtual disk into multiple files

   Splitting the disk makes it easier to move the virtual machine to another computer but
   may reduce performance with very large disks.

                              < Back   Next >   Cancel

Figure 5.8

The add hardware wizard will give the new disk file a name based on the name of the virtual machine. In my example, it wants to name it **Windows 11 Home-0.vmdk** but I like to change the name to match the size of the disk which makes it easier to distinguish when I have multiple disks on a VM. I will change the name to **Windows 11 Home-40.vmdk** so I will know it's my 40GB disk. I also like to click the Browse button to make sure that it's putting the hard disk file where I want it to go. It should place it with your other virtual machine files by default.

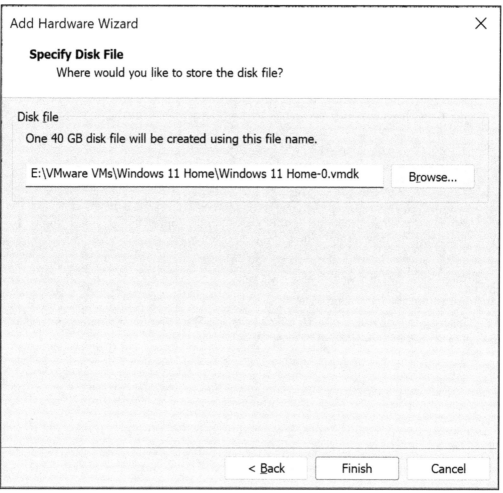

Figure 5.9

Figure 5.10 shows my virtual machine's hardware configuration after adding the new virtual disk. At the top right where it says *Disk file*, it shows the name that I gave it.

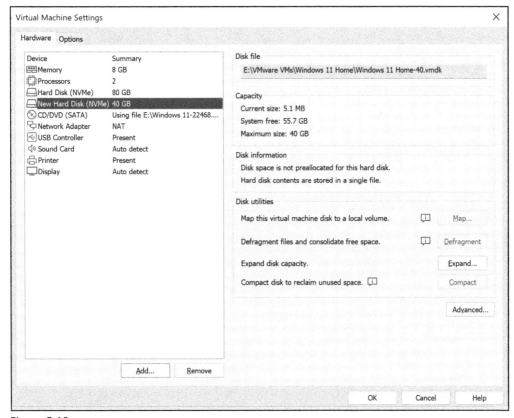

Figure 5.10

The process for adding other types of hardware is similar except you will have different choices and options depending on what type of hardware you are trying to add.

If you look at certain hardware devices, you will notice that there are checkboxes for Connected and Connect at power on. If you want this hardware to be active in your VM, make sure these boxes are checked.

VM Options

Next to the Hardware tab in the virtual machine settings, you will find a tab labeled Options. This section has many different settings that you can use to fine tune how your virtual machines are configured.

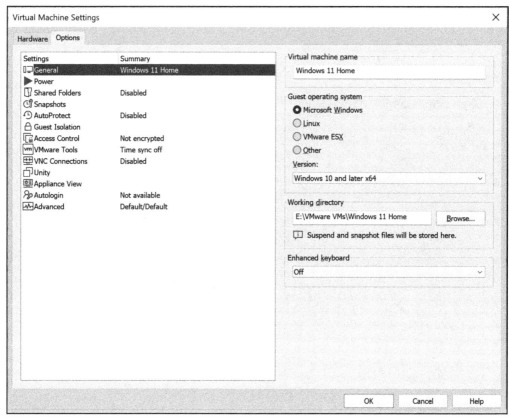

Figure 5.11

I will now take some time and go over all of the categories in the Options section.

- **General** – Here you can find general information about your virtual machine such as its name, operating system, version and the directory where the VM files are located.

- **Power** – If you need to change what power related actions are taken on your virtual machine such as closing it after powering off, you can do so here. You can also change the default power controls as needed.

Power options

☐ Enter full screen mode after powering on

☐ Close after powering off or suspending

☐ Report battery information to guest

Power controls

⬛	Shut Down Guest	⌄
⏸	Suspend Guest	⌄
▶	Start Up Guest	⌄
↻	Restart Guest	⌄

Figure 5.12

- **Shared Folders** – You might already know that you can drag and drop or copy and paste files between your host and guest VMs. But this needs to be done via the VM console so if you don't have it open then you can't do this. The shared folder option will let you share folders between the host and guest to copy files as needed. I will be going over this in more detail in chapter 8 along with how to map disk files from the guest to the host.

- **Snapshots** – One great thing about VMs is the ability to take a snapshot which is a point in time image of a virtual machine. Then if you need to revert back to that previous state of your VM, you can do so with a few clicks. I will be demonstrating snapshots in chapter 7 but here you can tell Workstation what to do with your snapshots when you shut down. The default is to just power off the VM and not do anything with any snapshots that you might have. If you don't use snapshots, then any changes you make here will not apply to your VM.

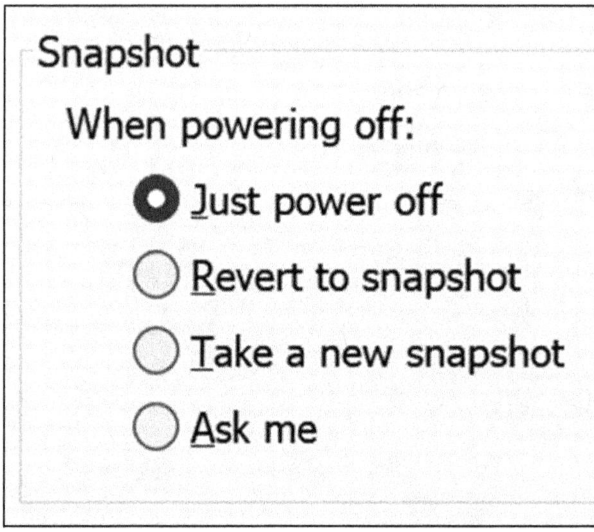

Snapshot

When powering off:

- ● <u>J</u>ust power off
- ○ <u>R</u>evert to snapshot
- ○ <u>T</u>ake a new snapshot
- ○ <u>A</u>sk me

Figure 5.13

- **AutoProtect** – Speaking of snapshots, the AutoProtect feature will take automatic snapshots of your virtual machine and the interval you specify. You can use this feature if you make regular changes to your virtual machine that might require you needing to roll back to an older version.

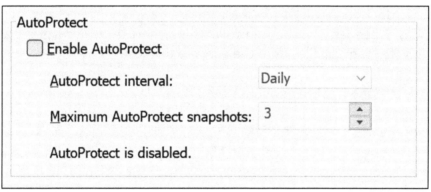

Figure 5.14

- **Guest Isolation** – One great feature of VMware Workstation is the ability to drag files from your host computer right to your guest computer as if it were the same computer. You can also copy and paste text and images just like you can between apps on your local computer.

  The *Share sensor input* options are used for tablet touch screen features such as when you have a laptop with a touchscreen. These won't do anything if you don't have a touchscreen but are still enabled by default.

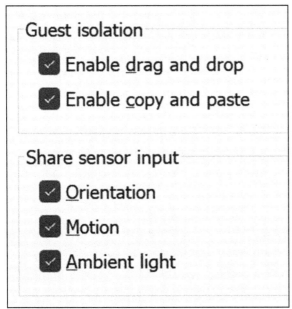

Figure 5.15

- **Access Control** – If you are planning on using your virtual machines for confidential purposes and need an extra layer of security then you can come and encrypt the VM. This will prevent users from accessing the VM via the console and changing any of its settings. When a VM is encrypted, you will need to enter the password you assigned to it even if you want to access it via VMware Workstation.

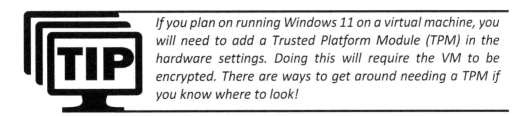

If you plan on running Windows 11 on a virtual machine, you will need to add a Trusted Platform Module (TPM) in the hardware settings. Doing this will require the VM to be encrypted. There are ways to get around needing a TPM if you know where to look!

- **VMware Tools** – This section allows you to change how VMware Tools are updated. The default is to update manually but you can change it to automatic.

- **VNC Connections** – If you don't want to use the console to access your virtual machines, you can setup a VNC (Virtual Network Computing) connection to use the guest computer. It's similar to Remote Desktop in Windows.

- **Unity** – If you like to toggle between your host computer and a guest VM and use applications on both, you might want to try Unity mode. This will display applications on the host system desktop as if they were running locally. Open programs from the VM in Unity mode appear on the Windows taskbar in the same way as open host programs. I will be going over this in more detail in chapter 8.

- **Appliance View** – This can be used if you are creating a VM that you will then export as an appliance so others can use it. You can add your name as the author and a version as well.

- **Autologin** – This can be used to have VMware automatically log into your computer with the name and password you use for your OS, so you don't have to type it in when you start the virtual machine. You will need to have VMware Tools installed to use this feature.

- **Advanced** – There are many settings in the Advanced section, and you will most likely never change any of them.

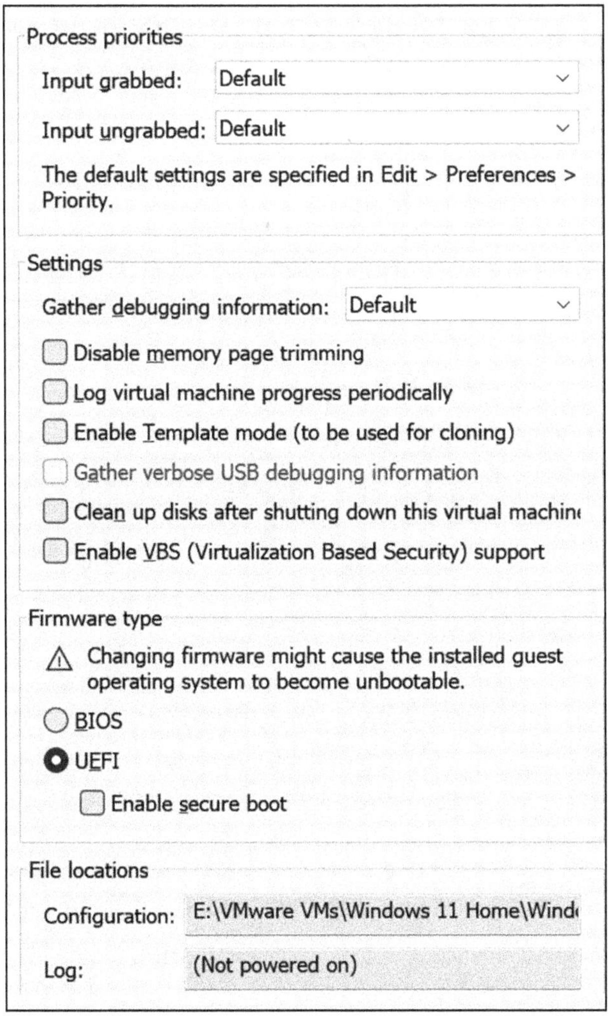

Process priorities

Input grabbed: Default ⌄

Input ungrabbed: Default ⌄

The default settings are specified in Edit > Preferences > Priority.

Settings

Gather debugging information: Default ⌄

☐ Disable memory page trimming
☐ Log virtual machine progress periodically
☐ Enable Template mode (to be used for cloning)
☐ Gather verbose USB debugging information
☐ Clean up disks after shutting down this virtual machine
☐ Enable VBS (Virtualization Based Security) support

Firmware type

⚠ Changing firmware might cause the installed guest operating system to become unbootable.

○ BIOS
● UEFI
☐ Enable secure boot

File locations

Configuration: E:\VMware VMs\Windows 11 Home\Windo

Log: (Not powered on)

Figure 5.16

Process priority settings are used to specify the priority that the Windows process scheduler gives to the VM. You can also find your firmware type here and change it if necessary. Just be sure to read the warning about how it might make your guest OS unbootable so only try it if you have no other option.

VM Power States

Since a virtual machine is technically a computer (running virtually), it makes sense that you should be able to change the power state just like you can with a physical computer.

If you select a VM you want to change the power state on and then click the power state button, you will see various options as shown in figure 5.17.

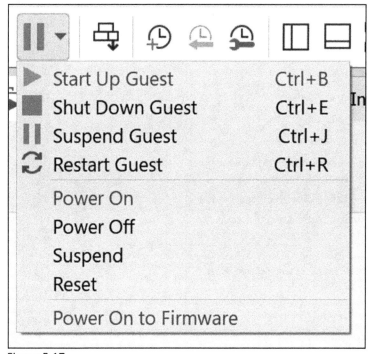

Figure 5.17

Even though most of these should be obvious, I will go over what each one will do.

- **Start Up Guest** – This will turn on a virtual machine that is powered off but will use a startup script via VMware Tools so the VM will use DHCP to get its IP address from Workstation.

- **Shut Down Guest** – Used to gracefully shut down a virtual machine by sending a shutdown signal to the guest OS.

- **Suspend Guest** – You can use this option to save the current state of a virtual machine OS and when you resume the VM, the programs that were running before you suspended it will resume as you left them. This also uses a script that will run via VMware Tools.

- **Restart Guest** – Used to gracefully shut down and then restart a virtual machine by sending a restart signal to the guest OS.

- **Power On** – This will simply turn on the virtual machine.

- **Power Off** – This will simply turn off the power as if you pulled the plug or pressed the power button.

- **Suspend** – This will only suspend the VM state itself.

- **Reset** – Resetting a VM is like pressing the reset button on your PC. It will do a hard reset and not shutdown the OS first.

- **Power On to Firmware** – Even though a VM is not a physical computer, you can still go into its BIOS\UEFI settings to do things like change the boot order like you can on a physical PC.

Updating Hardware Compatibility

When creating a virtual machine, you saw that you can choose the hardware compatibility during the process. Once you choose the compatibility level, it stays with the VM until you change it.

When you upgrade your VMware Workstation software, you can then upgrade your virtual machines to match the level of the software so they can take advantage of any additional features that are available with the new version.

To update the hardware compatibility of a VM, select that virtual machine and go to the *VM* menu, then *Manage* and finally click on *Change Hardware Compatibility*. This will launch the *Change Hardware Compatibility Wizard* where you can simply click on the *Next* button.

Figure 5.18

Then you can choose the hardware compatibility level you want to apply to your virtual machine. As you can see in figure 5.19, you can also change it to an older version if you have a reason to do so. It will also show you what products are compatible and also what features are available in each version.

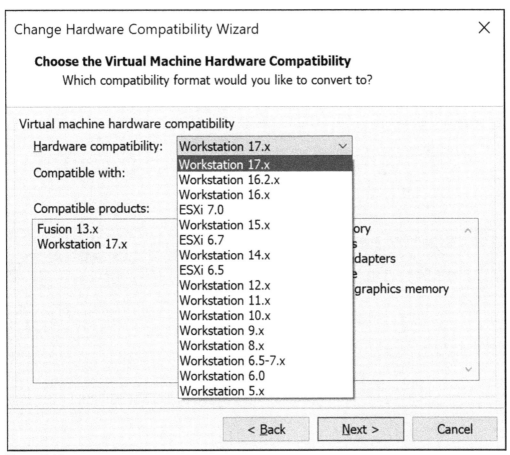

Figure 5.19

Once you select your version and click on the *Next* button, you will be asked if you want to make a clone of the VM and have the new hardware level applied or if you want to apply it to the existing virtual machine. The reason to make a clone is to make sure you don't have any issues with the new hardware level before applying it to your main VM. I always choose the *Alter this virtual machine* choice and have never had a problem.

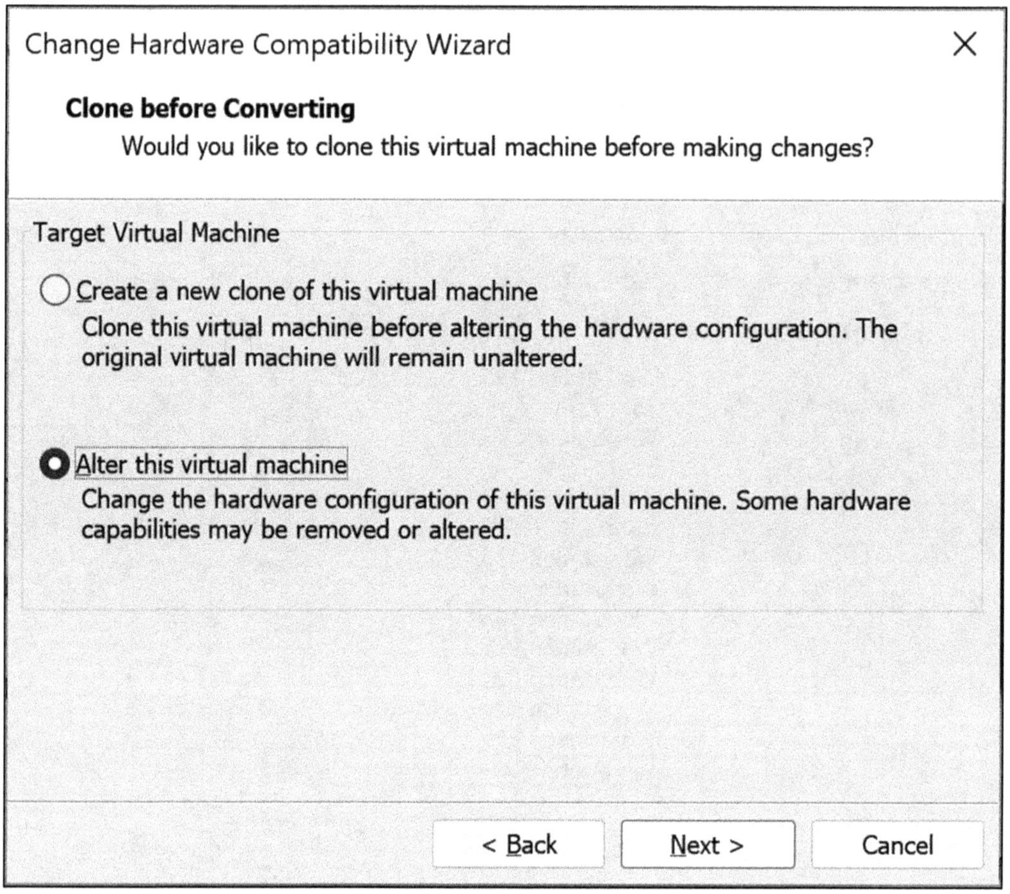

Change Hardware Compatibility Wizard   ✕

Clone before Converting
      Would you like to clone this virtual machine before making changes?

Target Virtual Machine

○ Create a new clone of this virtual machine
    Clone this virtual machine before altering the hardware configuration. The
    original virtual machine will remain unaltered.

● Alter this virtual machine
    Change the hardware configuration of this virtual machine. Some hardware
    capabilities may be removed or altered.

                              < Back   Next >   Cancel

Figure 5.20

Then you will click on the *Next* button again and the process will run, and you will
be shown the results (figures 5.21 & 5.22).

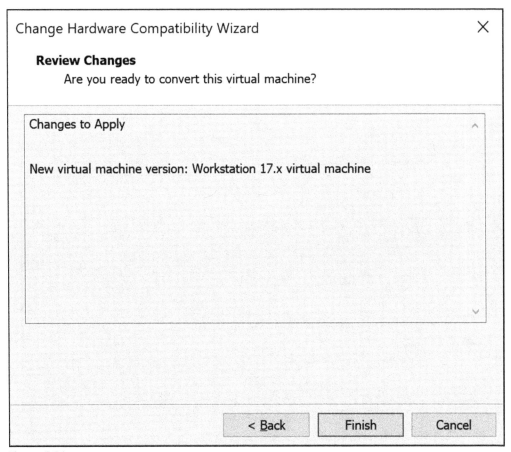

Figure 5.21

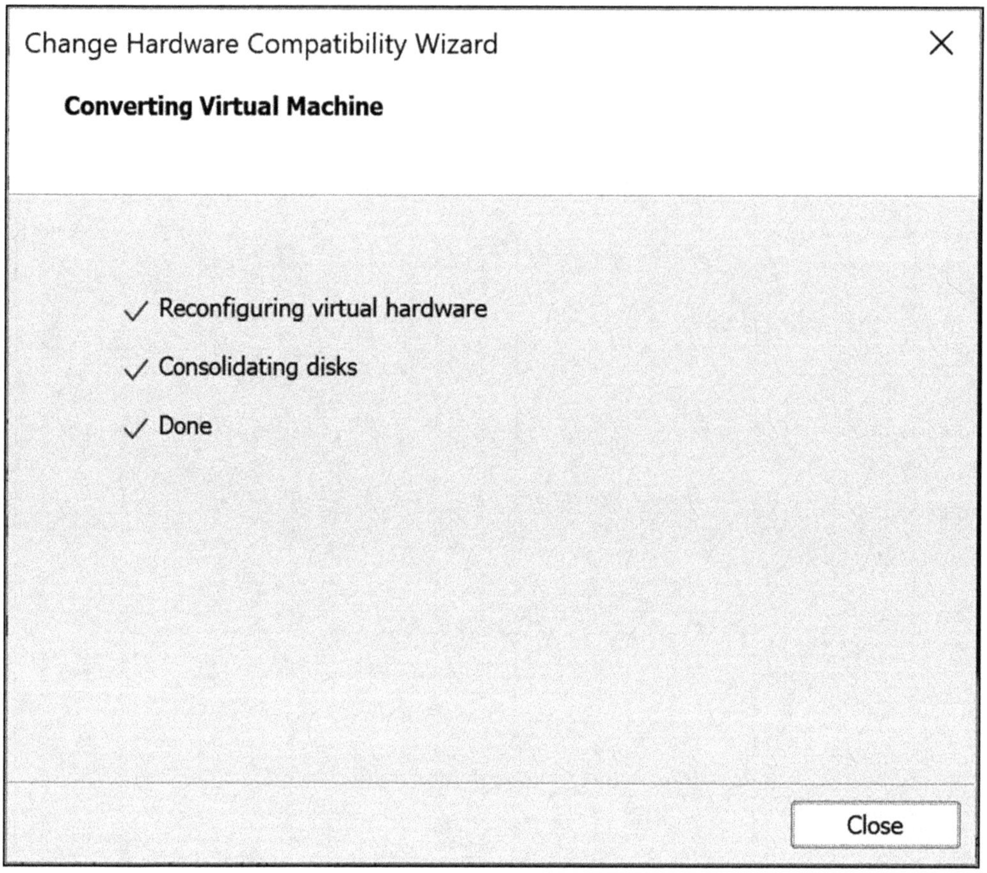

Change Hardware Compatibility Wizard   ✕

Converting Virtual Machine

✓ Reconfiguring virtual hardware

✓ Consolidating disks

✓ Done

Close

Figure 5.22

Chapter 6 – Networking

Even though your virtual machines are all running on your host computer, they still use networking to communicate with each other and with your host if needed. And of course to get out to the internet, they need a network connection as well since your host computer is the device that is providing that network connection.

By default, when you install Windows and most other operating systems, the computer will use DHCP (Dynamic Host Configuration Protocol) to obtain an IP address from a DHCP server. In a physical world without virtualization, your computer would get its IP address from another computer running as a DHCP server or even something like a router that has a DHCP server built in. For VMware Workstation, virtual machines get their IP addresses from the DHCP server that comes built into the software.

DHCP Settings
VMware Workstation has some default DHCP settings for the built in networks that come preconfigured with the software. Usually you will see two Host-only networks and one NAT network configured in the settings. I will be getting into more detail on both of these later in the chapter.

If you open the *Virtual Network Editor* from the *Edit* menu, you will see the networks that are configured for you (figure 6.1). As you can see, the box that says *Use local DHCP service to distribute IP addresses to VMs* is checked by default and is also greyed out. To change this you would need to click on the button that says *Change Settings* at the bottom right.

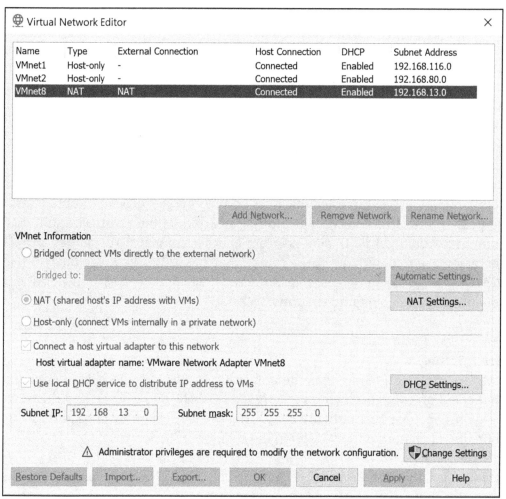

Figure 6.1

If you click on the DHCP Settings button, you will see the subnet and subnet mask used for this DHCP range. You will also be shown the starting and ending IP addresses that will be available to your virtual machines. These values can be changed as well using the Change Settings button.

DHCP Settings   ✕

Network: vmnet8

Subnet IP: 192.168.13.0

Subnet mask: 255.255.255.0

Starting IP address: 192 . 168 . 13 . 128

Ending IP address: 192 . 168 . 13 . 254

Broadcast address: 192.168.13.255

	Days:	Hours:	Minutes:
Default lease time:	0	0	30
Max lease time:	0	2	0

                      OK   Cancel   Help

Figure 6.2

So if you were to do an ipconfig from a command prompt on a virtual machine, you should get an IP address within that range.

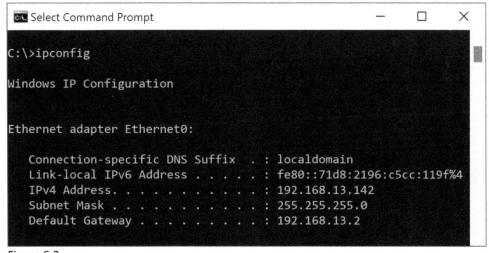

Figure 6.3

VMnet Adapters

Your host communicates with your virtual machines via virtual network adapters that are automatically configured on your host when you install VMware Workstation.

If you were to look at your configured network adapters on your host, you would see something similar to figure 6.4. I also have a network adapter for VirtualBox since I have their virtualization software installed on the same host computer.

If you would like to learn how to use the free Oracle VirtualBox virtualization software, then check out my book titled **VirtualBox Made Easy.**
https://www.amazon.com/dp/1654146242

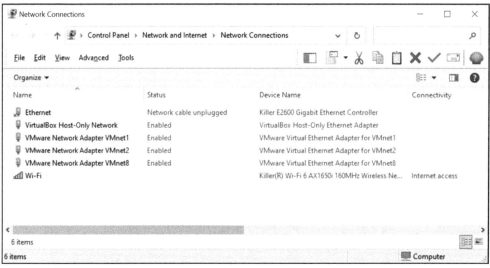

Figure 6.4

You can see I have three VMnet adapters and they match up with what you will see in the Virtual Network Editor (VMnet 1, 2 and 8).

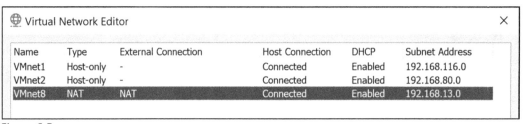

Name	Type	External Connection	Host Connection	DHCP	Subnet Address
VMnet1	Host-only	-	Connected	Enabled	192.168.116.0
VMnet2	Host-only	-	Connected	Enabled	192.168.80.0
VMnet8	NAT	NAT	Connected	Enabled	192.168.13.0

Figure 6.5

If you do an *Ipconfig* command on your host computer, you will also see these VMnet adapters with their associated IP addresses.

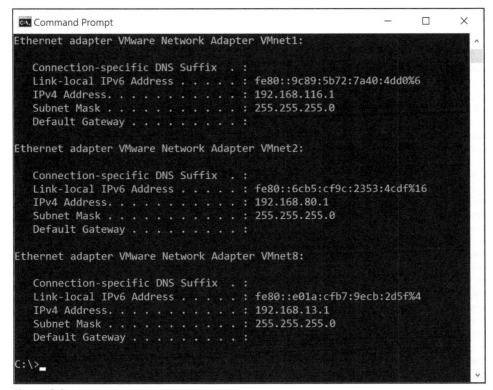

Figure 6.6

If you need to configure additional networks on your host, you can add more networks using the preconfigured VMnet adapters as needed. You will need to go back to the Virtual Network Editor, click the Change Settings button and then click on the *Add Network* button.

Next, you will choose one of the VMnet adapters and click the *OK* button.

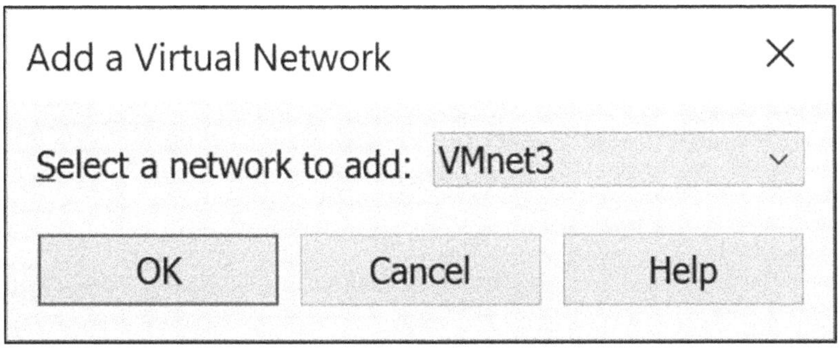

Figure 6.7

Then back in the Virtual Network Editor you can then choose the network type and change the DHCP range if needed. Then once everything is configured you will click the *Apply* button. I will be discussing the various network types next.

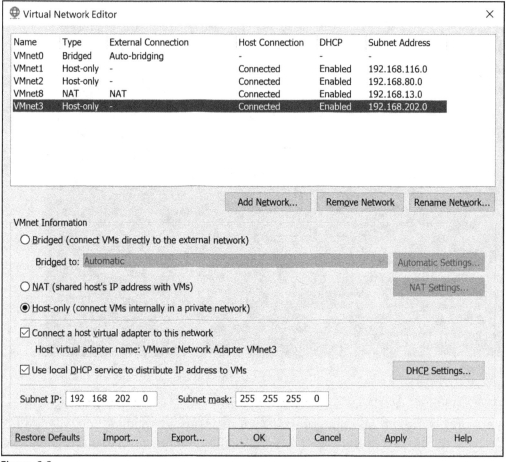

Figure 6.8

Now when you go to the network adapter settings of a virtual machine and choose *Custom*, you will see your new network configured with its corresponding VMnet adapter.

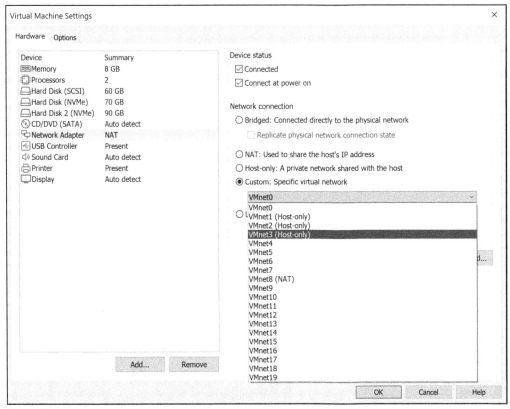

Figure 6.9

You can also add an additional network adapter to a virtual machine and then assign it to your new network in case you still need the exiting network to be in place.

NAT (Network Address Translation)

The default network type for new virtual machines is to use NAT. This is used so your VM can communicate over the internet using the network card and internet connection from your host computer.

NAT works by mapping (or translating) the IP address of your internet public address to multiple private IP addresses so that all of your virtual machines can use the same internet connection via your host. On your home network, the NAT process is usually taken care of by your router.

When it comes to communicating with other virtual machines or the host computer, here is what NAT will allow you to do.

- The VM can communicate with other VMs on the NAT network.
- The VM can communicate with the host computer.
- The host computer can communicate with the VM.
- The VM can communicate with other hosts on my host network, but these hosts can't initiate communications with the VM.

Bridged Connection

If you need to have your virtual machine have direct access to your external network, then you can create a bridged network. One thing to keep in mind is that your VM will need an IP address from the external network to be able to communicate. Once this is setup, other computers on your network will be able to communicate directly with the virtual machine.

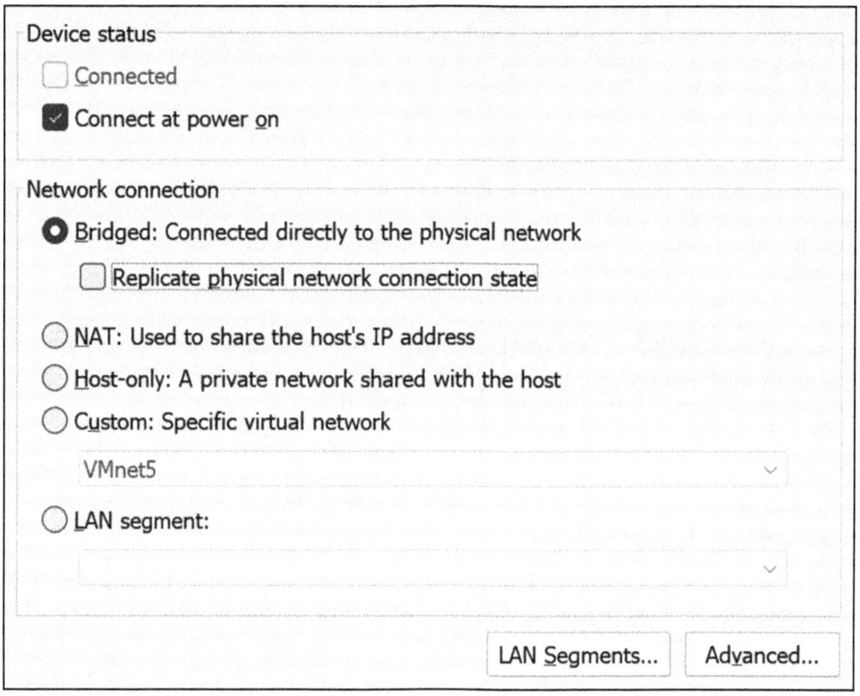

Figure 6.10

When you used a bridged connection, Workstation will assign the VMnet0 network adapter to the VM and will get its IP address from the local area network (LAN). Then the VM can talk to the other VMs, as well as any hosts on the LAN network. Plus the other hosts in your LAN will also be able to communicate with this virtual machine.

The *Replicate physical network connection state* checkbox is used for mobile devices such as a laptop. When you use this option, the IP address of the VM is automatically renewed as you transition from one wired or wireless network to another.

Host-Only Network
If you only need network communication between your host and a specific virtual machine or machines, you can configure the host-only network type. Host-only networking will give you a network connection between the VM its configured on and the host computer. It will use a virtual network adapter that is visible to the host OS. This provides you with an isolated network between your host and VM(s).

Once you have this configured, the virtual machine will only be able to communicate with the host computer and any other virtual machines that are configured for this host-only network.

If you have more than one host-only network configured and plan on using it with more than one VM, make sure you select the same network for both virtual machines.

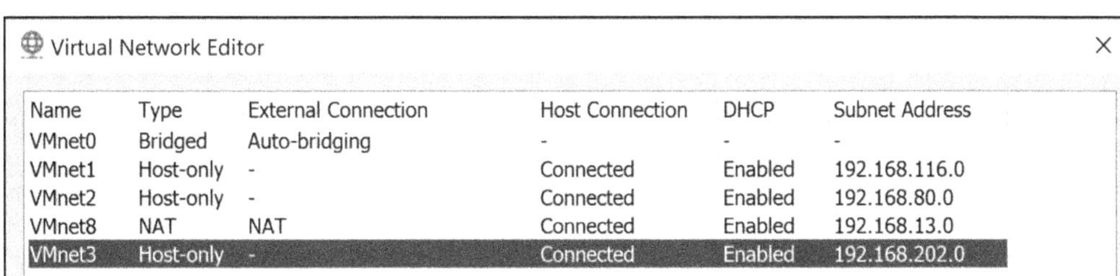

Name	Type	External Connection	Host Connection	DHCP	Subnet Address
VMnet0	Bridged	Auto-bridging	-	-	-
VMnet1	Host-only	-	Connected	Enabled	192.168.116.0
VMnet2	Host-only	-	Connected	Enabled	192.168.80.0
VMnet8	NAT	NAT	Connected	Enabled	192.168.13.0
VMnet3	Host-only	-	Connected	Enabled	192.168.202.0

Virtual Network Editor ×

Figure 6.11

LAN Segments
If you really need to isolate your virtual machines from the rest of the network… or the world, you can setup a LAN segment to accomplish this. LAN segments are not as commonly used but they are a great way to do things such as test software or settings that might have a negative effect on your network or networked computers if they were connected.
To create a LAN segment simply click on the *LAN Segments* button and then click on Add, type in your LAN segment name and click on OK. Then you will be able

to select that LAN segment from the dropdown list. In my example, I named my segment *Private*.

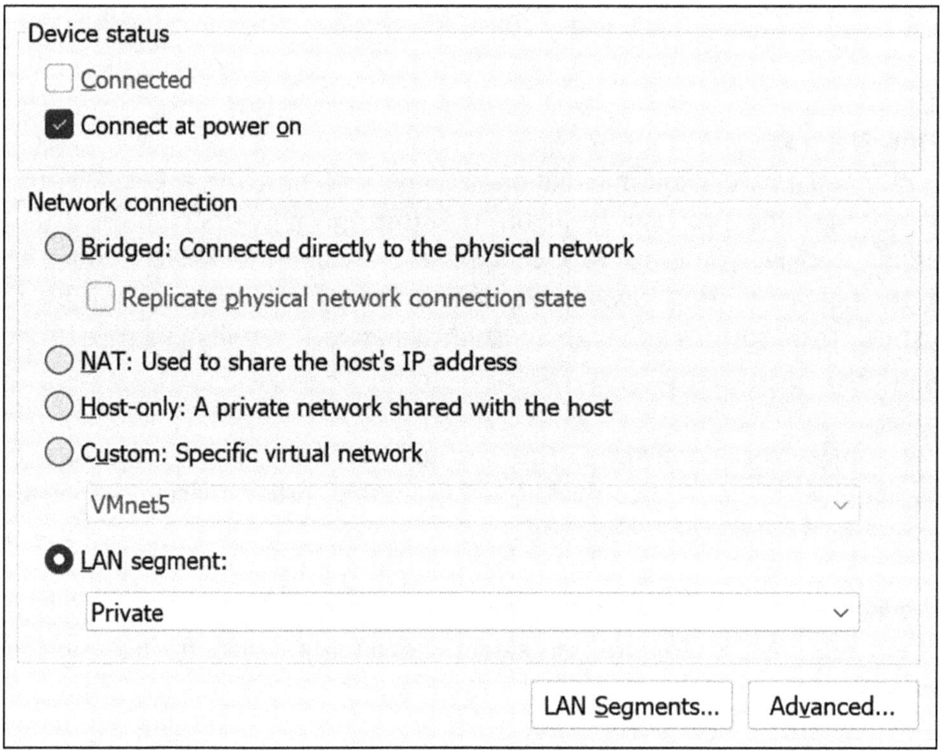

Figure 6.12

Then any VMs that you configure to use the LAN segment will not be able to communicate with the host or other virtual machines unless they are in the same LAN segment.

Chapter 7 – Snapshots & Cloning

One of the best parts about using virtual machines is their flexibility when it comes to backing things up, reversing changes simply being able to make a copy of a VM as needed. Also, don't forget how easy it is to simply start over again if you make a mess of your guest computer.

In this chapter, I will be discussing two methods you can use to give yourself some insurance when it comes to your virtual machines. I have mentioned that it's very easy to just recreate a VM if something goes terribly wrong but sometimes you have a lot of work that was put into one of your guests and you need a way to ensure that you can recover that work if something goes wrong.

Virtual Machine Snapshots
Snapshots are used to capture the state of a virtual machine at a specific point in time and then preserve it so it can be reverted back to at a later date if needed. Let's say you were going to install some new software that might be harmful to your VM, and you wanted to have a way to revert back to the way the computer was before installing the software. These snapshots include the contents of the VM's memory, its settings, and the state of all the virtual disks.

To accomplish this, you can create a snapshot of the virtual machine before installing the software to make sure you have a working copy of the VM in case something goes wrong during your software testing, and maybe uninstalling the software might not fix the problem. You can also have multiple snapshots taken at different points in time allowing you several ways to restore your virtual machine if needed.

Since taking a snapshot captures the entire state of a virtual machine, it will take up room on your host computer. These snapshots are stored in the same location as the other virtual machine files, and you can recognize them by the word snapshot after the VM name the file name. Figure 7.1 shows the four files used by two snapshots.

Windows 11 Insider-1.vmdk
Windows 11 Insider-1-000001.vmdk
Windows 11 Insider-1-000002.vmdk
Windows 11 Insider-000002.vmdk
Windows 11 Insider-Snapshot1.vmem
Windows 11 Insider-Snapshot1.vmsn
Windows 11 Insider-Snapshot2.vmem
Windows 11 Insider-Snapshot2.vmsn
7.27 GB
Computer

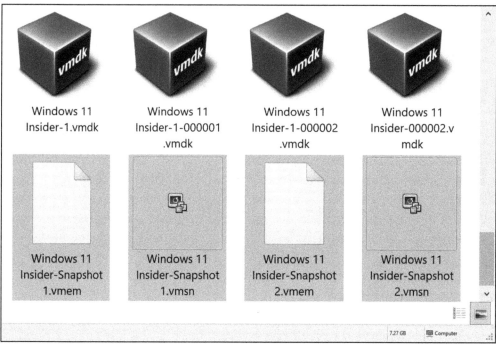

Figure 7.1

To create a snapshot, you can select a VM, click on the VM menu and choose *Snapshot > Take a Snapshot*. You should then give the snapshot a name and maybe even a date, so you know exactly when it was taken and you can also add a description if you think you need more detail.

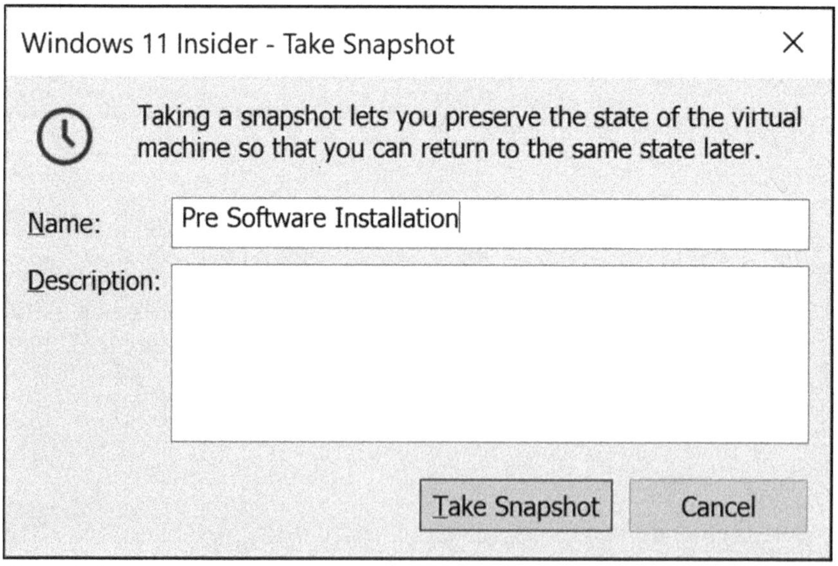

Windows 11 Insider - Take Snapshot
Taking a snapshot lets you preserve the state of the virtual machine so that you can return to the same state later.
Name:
Pre Software Installation
Description:
Take Snapshot
Cancel

Figure 7.2

The amount of time the snapshot takes will depend on the size of your VM but it's usually fairly quick.

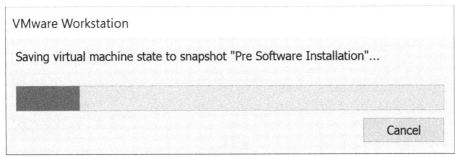

Figure 7.3

Once the snapshot has been created, you can go back to the Snapshot menu and see the option to revert it (roll it back), or you can click on *Snapshot Manager* to be taken to the console where you will be able to manage your snapshots (figure 7.5).

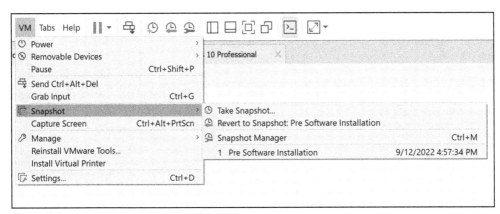

Figure 7.4

The section that says *You Are Here* indicates the present state of the virtual machine. You can then take another snapshot if needed or even clone the current state of the VM.

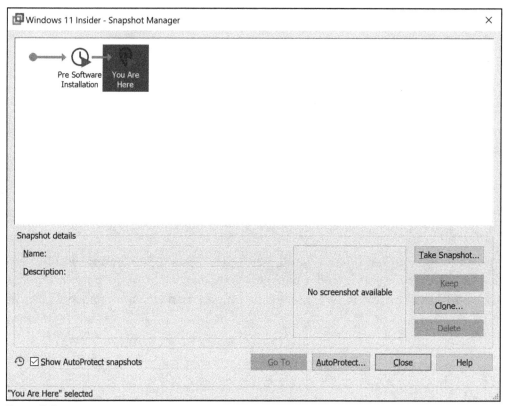

Figure 7.5

I will now make a second snapshot called *After First Test* and figure 7.6 shows both of my snapshots and the order they were taken.

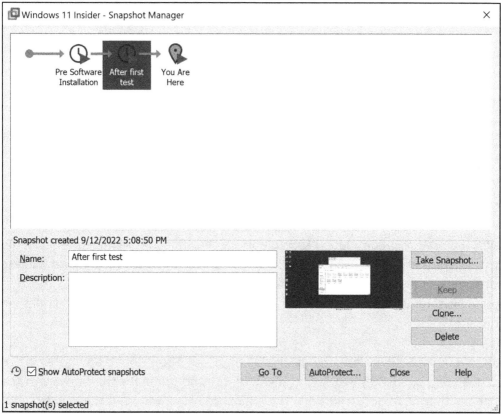

Figure 7.6

Now if I need to revert back to one of these snapshots, I can select it and then click on the *Go To* button. I want to go back to the first snapshot called Pre Software Installation so I will choose that one and click on Go To. I will then get a message telling me that the current state of my VM will be lost so anything I have worked on since I took this snapshot will be gone.

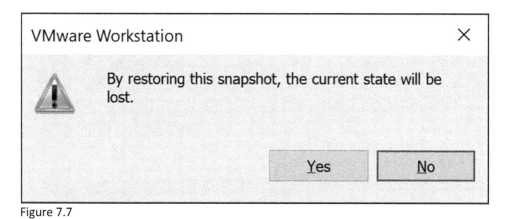

Figure 7.7

I will then be shown the status of the snapshot restoration.

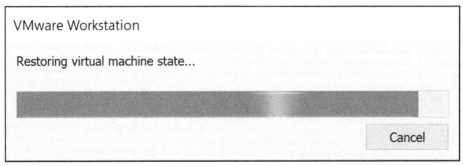

Figure 7.8

After the restore is complete, I can go back to the Snapshot Manager and see the current state of my virtual machine. As you can see in figure 7.9, I am at the Pre Software Installation point, but I still have the option to revert to the After first test snapshot which is technically newer than the Pre Software Installation snapshot.

And of course I can delete any particular snapshot I don't need anymore. When you delete a snapshot, Workstation will merge the original virtual disk with the changes that have occurred since the snapshot was created. If there were a lot of changes, the merging process could take a while.

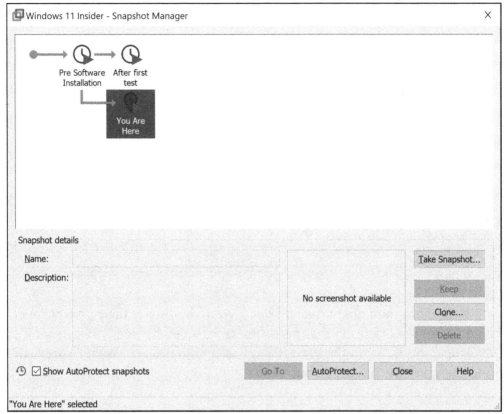

Figure 7.9

If you go to the settings of your virtual machine to the *Options* tab, you will see a section called *Snapshots* where you can set some additional options regarding your VM snapshots.

The default setting for snapshots when shutting down the VM is to just power it off and not do anything involving snapshots. There are other options such as reverting the VM to a snapshot or taking a new snapshot every time you power off the virtual machine. You can also set it to ask you what you want to do with your snapshots when you shut down your VM.

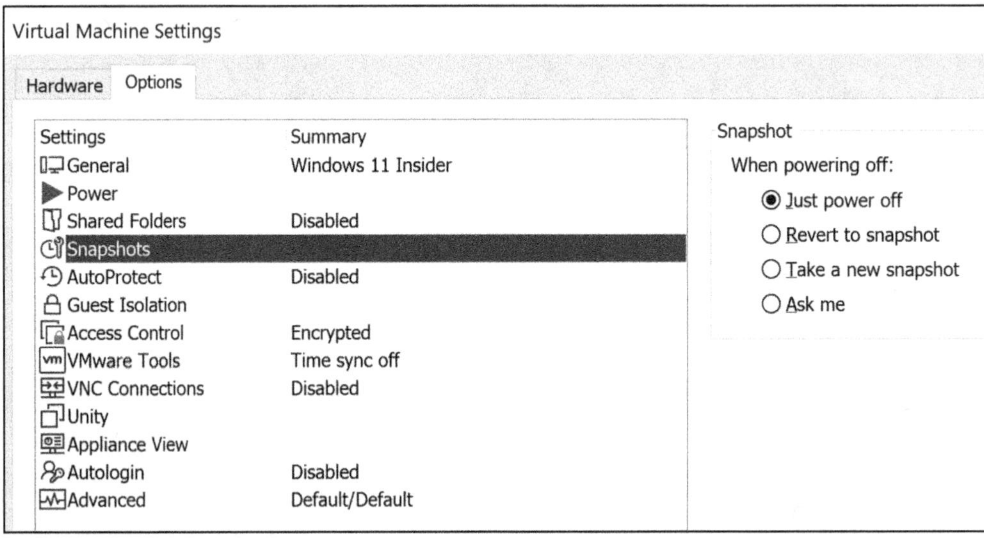

Virtual Machine Settings

Hardware   Options

Settings	Summary
General	Windows 11 Insider
Power	
Shared Folders	Disabled
Snapshots	
AutoProtect	Disabled
Guest Isolation	
Access Control	Encrypted
VMware Tools	Time sync off
VNC Connections	Disabled
Unity	
Appliance View	
Autologin	Disabled
Advanced	Default/Default

Snapshot

When powering off:

- ◉ Just power off
- ○ Revert to snapshot
- ○ Take a new snapshot
- ○ Ask me

Figure 7.10

If you have more than one virtual disk in a VM that you are taking snapshots of and don't want the data on that particular disk to be affected, you can set it to *Independent* mode. From the VM settings, select the disk you want to apply this to and then click the *Advanced* button.

Next, you will need to check the box for *Independent* so that the disk will not be affected by snapshots. There is one other setting you need to choose which will apply to this virtual disk whether you use snapshots or not. *Persistent* mode will write any changes you make to the disk such as when you save a file. *Nonpersistent* will discard any changes you make to the disk so if you add files for example and then shut down the VM, they will be gone the next time you start it up.

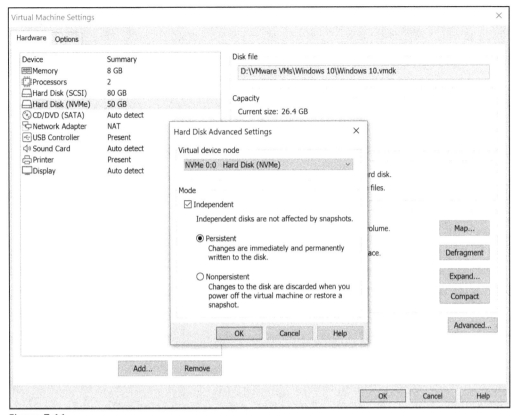

Figure 7.11

AutoProtect Snapshots

VMware Workstation offers a way to automatically take snapshots of your virtual machines at specific intervals, so you don't need to remember to do it yourself. You can sort of think of this as a way to backup your virtual machines even though snapshots are not really considered a backup method.

To enable AutoProtect snapshots, go to the virtual machine's settings and then to the Options tab. Next, you will click on the AutoProtect section on the left and check the box next to *Enable AutoProtect*.

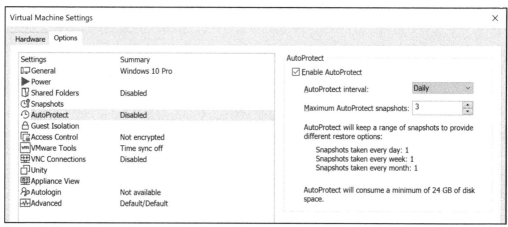

Figure 7.12

Now you can choose from daily, hourly, or half-hourly snapshot intervals. You can also specify the maximum amount of AutoProtect snapshots you want to keep. Once the maximum is reached, the oldest snapshot will be deleted when the next one is created.

The AutoProtect snapshot feature will only work when the virtual machine is powered on so keep that in mind if you plan on using it. And because of this, you cannot clone an AutoProtect snapshot and can only clone the VM when it's powered off.

Cloning a Virtual Machine
Another great thing about virtualization is the ability to make duplicates, or clones of your virtual machines. Sure you can clone your hard drive in your physical computer and then install it in another computer to make a duplicate but that takes much more time... and money!

Cloning is the process of making a copy of a virtual machine so you can do whatever you need to on it without risking harming the original. It's also a good way to make multiple copies of a configured VM so you don't have to do the same process over and over. You can just configure one virtual machine exactly the way you need it. And then make as many clones of that VM as needed. Of course you have the issue of duplicate computer names, IP addresses and SIDs (security identifiers) which can cause problems for Windows computers on a domain.

You can create clones of the virtual machine itself or you can create a clone of that VM from a snapshot. This means the clone will be a copy of how the VM was configured when that snapshot was created and not the current state of the VM.

There are two main types of clones that you need to be aware of, full clones and linked clones. Linked clones can be a bit confusing as to how they work so many people just stick with using full clones.

Full Clones
When you create a full clone, you are making an independent copy of the source virtual machine and once the clone is created, it's a completely separate VM. Full clones take longer to create and have better performance than linked clones. They will also be larger in size and can't use snapshots that were made on the parent (source) VM.

Linked Clones
A linked clone is a copy of a virtual machine that shares the virtual disks with the parent VM. A linked clone must have access to the parent VM, or it will stop working. You can have multiple linked clones that use the same parent VM. These linked clones are created from snapshots of the parents.

When you create a linked clone, it will have access to the software and files that were on the parent when it was created. After it is created, changes to the disk on the parent do not affect the linked clone and changes to the linked clone do not affect the parent. Be aware that you cannot delete a linked clone snapshot without destroying the linked clone.

Creating a Clone
To create a clone of a virtual machine, you will first need to power it off otherwise you will get a message saying it can't be created until you do unless you are making a clone from a snapshot that was created when the VM was powered off. In other words, there are three ways to go about making a snapshot.

1. You can create a clone of a VM that doesn't have any snapshots if it's powered off.

2. You can create a clone of a VM from a snapshot state that was made when the VM was on, but the VM has to be off to make the clone.

3. You can create a clone of a VM from a snapshot state that was made when the VM was off, and this can be done with the VM on or off.

To create a clone, select the virtual machine you want to clone and go to the VM menu and then choose *Manage > Clone*.

You will know if you have any cloneable snapshots that were made when the virtual machine was off when you start the clone wizard. Figure 7.13 shows what happens when you don't have a cloneable snapshot. You can see the second option for *An existing snapshot* is greyed out.

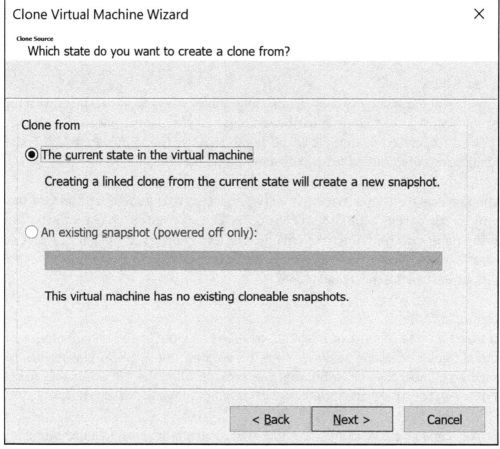

Figure 7.13

Figure 7.14 shows how things will look if you do have a cloneable snapshot because you will be able to select it from the list.

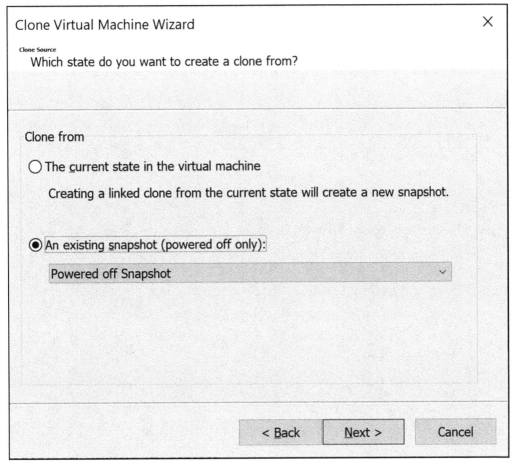

Figure 7.14

For my example, I will be creating a clone from the current state of the virtual machine itself and not a snapshot but just wanted you to be aware that you can create clones from snapshots if needed.

When I run the clone wizard it asks for the name you want to use for your cloned virtual machine. I will stick with the default name and location, but you can change these if needed.

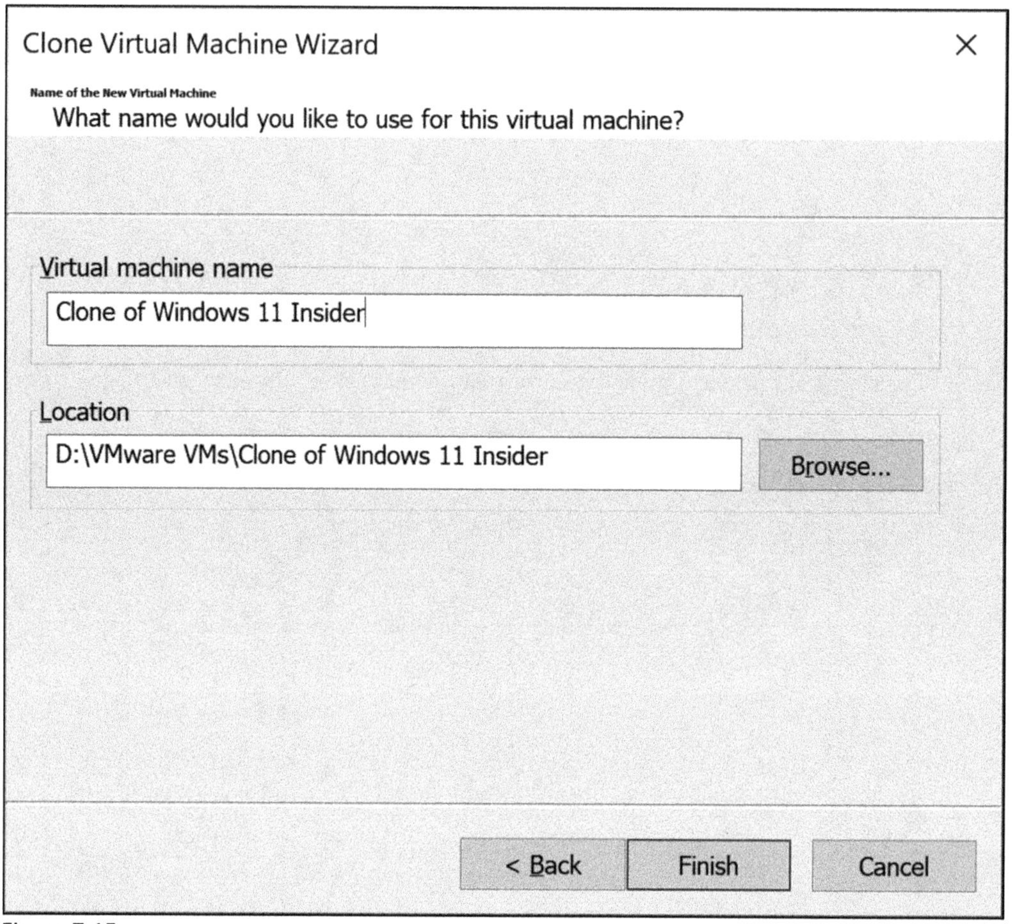

Clone Virtual Machine Wizard   ✕

Name of the New Virtual Machine
What name would you like to use for this virtual machine?

Virtual machine name

Clone of Windows 11 Insider

Location

D:\VMware VMs\Clone of Windows 11 Insider   Browse...

< Back   Finish   Cancel

Figure 7.15

Once the cloning process begins, you will see a status bar with the progress. If your virtual machine is large or had multiple virtual disks, this process can take a bit of time.

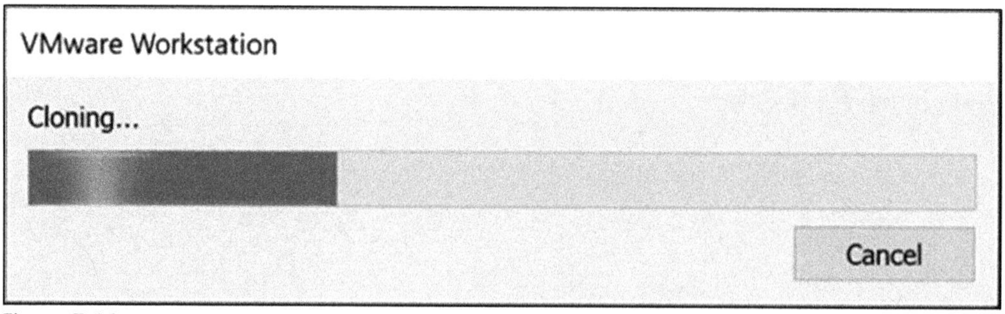

VMware Workstation

Cloning...

Cancel

Figure 7.16

Now that my clone has been created, I can power it on and use it just like it was the original VM. Any changes I make to the clone will only apply to the clone itself and will not affect the source VM.

If I compare the size of the files from my original VM (left) to the clone (right), I can see that the original is larger. This is because the snapshots from the original did not transfer over to the clone.

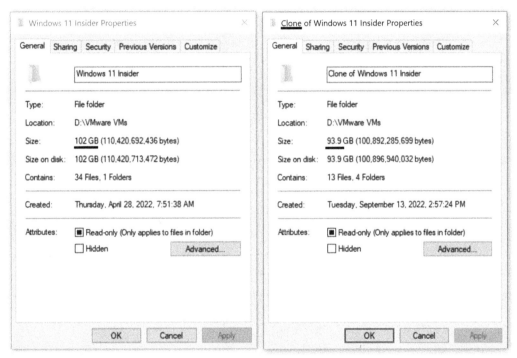

Figure 7.17

Now I will delete all of the snapshots from the original VM and as you can see in figure 7.18, the file sizes are much closer now between the two virtual machines.

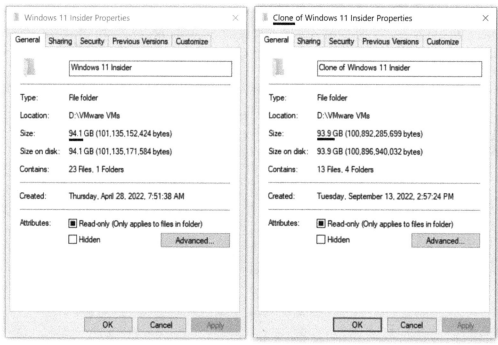

Figure 7.18

When I go to my virtual machine library, I can see both my original VM (Windows 11 Insider) and my clone underneath it and use either one independently of the other (figure 7.19). If I decide I no longer need my clone, I can simply delete it and once again, it will not affect the original virtual machine.

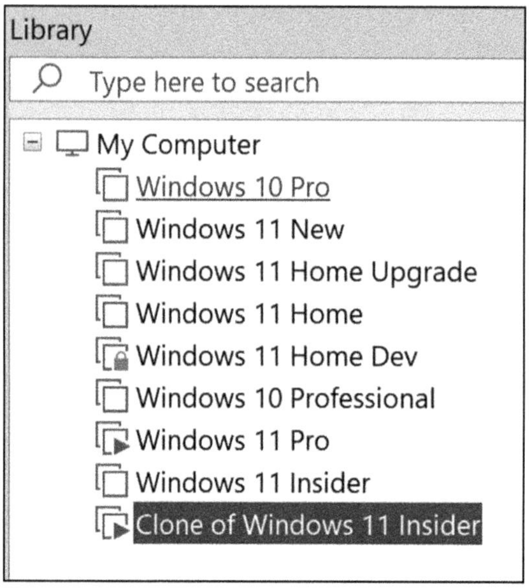

Figure 7.19

Chapter 8 – Preferences & Extras

Now that you have a solid understanding of how virtualization works, hopefully you have tried creating some virtual machines, played with the hardware settings and installed an operating system on them.

There are other features of VMware Workstation that you will discover as you browse around the menus and start investigating the settings. In this chapter, I will be covering some additional configuration options and going over some extra features that you will most likely find very handy.

VMware Workstation Preferences
So far, I have shown you the hardware settings and options for individual virtual machines, but now I want to go over the preferences for the VMware Workstation software itself. There are many things you can change here and most of them you probably never need to adjust, but it's nice to know how to get to these settings if needed.

Figure 8.1 shows all of the available preference settings and as you can see, there are many categories to choose from. You can get to preferences from the *Edit* menu. If you would like to get more information about any of these preferences, click on the *Help* button while on that setting and you will be taken to the VMware website to the help page for that item.

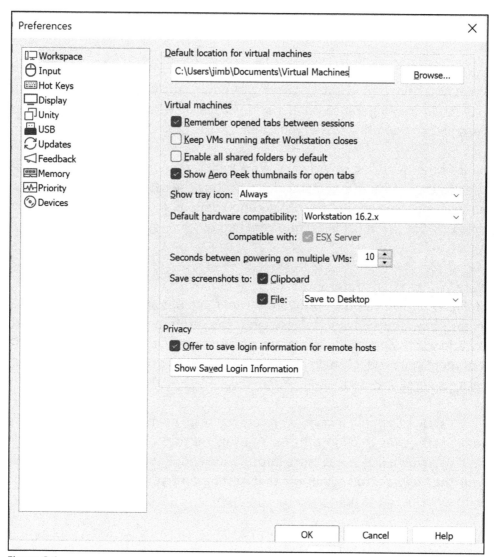

Figure 8.1

Rather than discuss each section in detail, I will summarize what you can do from each category and then you can go check things out and poke around yourself.

- **Workspace** – Here you will find general settings for your virtual machine workspace. One thing I like to change is the default location for virtual machines as you can see at the top of figure 8.1. All of the other settings I like to leave at their defaults.

- **Input** – The input section has to do with how your mouse and keyboard interact with the virtual machine. By default, when you click inside the VM console window, the mouse and keyboard control switches to the VM rather than your host computer.

The *Cursor* section shows you what will happen with the mouse as you move your mouse in and out of the virtual machine console. If you have VMware Tools installed, you can move in and out of the console back to the host computer. If you don't have VMware Tools installed, you will need to press Ctrl-Alt to give mouse control back to the host.

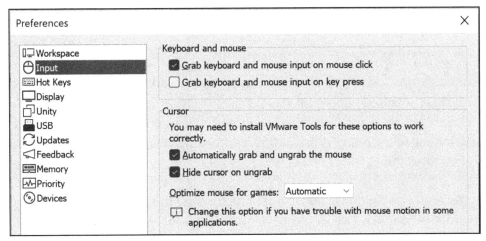

Figure 8.2

- **Hot Keys** – Just like with most other Windows applications, Workstation has keyboard combinations known as hot keys that allow you to perform an action by pressing that key combination rather than having to find the menu item or button with your mouse. If you click on any of the buttons in this setting (Ctrl, Shift, Alt or Win), the hot key combinations will change so you can choose which key combination works the best for you.

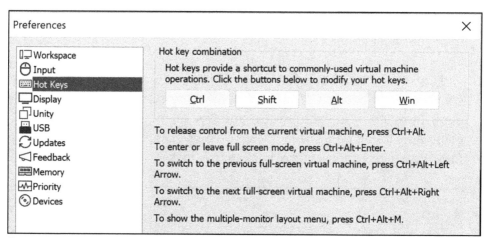

Figure 8.3

- **Display** – This section contains settings for how your VM console window is displayed on your host. For example, when you make a virtual machine window full screen, Workstation can change the resolution of the VM to match so things look correct and to scale.

  You can also do things such as change the way the menu and toolbar buttons work. And if you like to use dark mode for your Windows apps, you can set Workstation to match your theme.

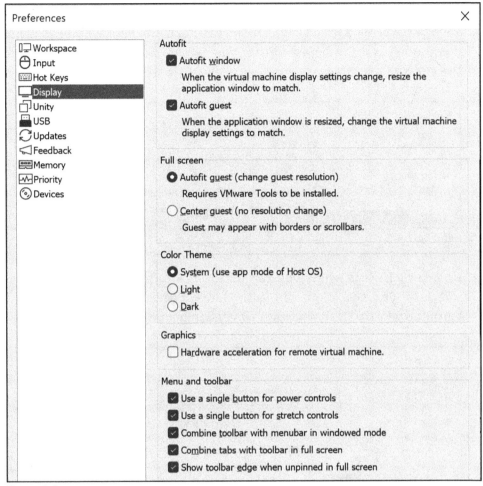

Figure 8.4

- **Unity** – Unity is used to display apps that are running in your virtual machine on your desktop. I will be discussing this more later in the chapter but here you can set the hot key for this feature.

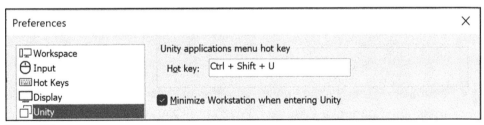

Figure 8.5

- **USB** – Once you start using VMware Workstation on a regular basis, you will start to notice that when you attach a USB device to your host computer,

- Workstation will ask you if you want to attach it to the host or to a guest VM. Then you will need to tell it which one to attach it to before you can continue. If you don't want to be asked this, you can have it default to the host or to the guest.

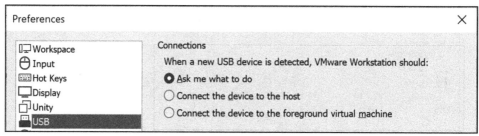

Figure 8.6

- **Updates** – Here is where you can decide how often Workstation checks for software updates. You can also have VMware Tools for your VMs automatically updated when a new version becomes available.

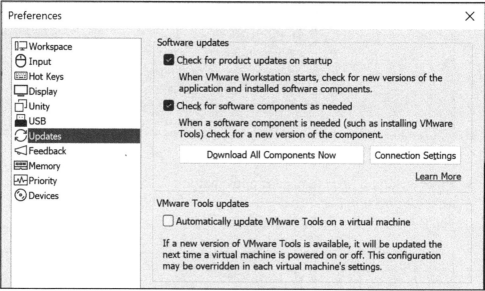

Figure 8.7

- **Feedback** – This section gives you the opportunity to join the VMware Customer Experience Feedback Program if you want to voice your opinion on things you like or don't like about VMware Workstation.

- **Memory** – This is an important section to check out because the setting here is used to reserve a set amount of the RAM from your host to be used for virtual machines. So if this number is too high compared to the total amount of RAM installed in your host computer, you might start to run into performance issues with your host and your guests. The host in this example only has 32GB of RAM and Workstation is reserving 28GB for all of the running VMs. Ideally you would have 16 or more GB of RAM to avoid having memory issues.

The *Additional memory* section is where you can have Workstation use your hard drive as swap space for memory when your actual RAM memory is getting low.

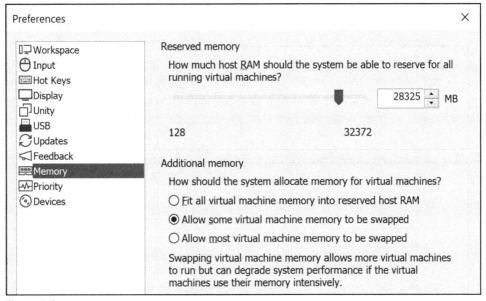

Figure 8.8

- **Priority** – Here you can adjust VM process priority when their keyboard and mouse input is grabbed. The default is *Normal,* but you can set this to *High* if needed.

The *Snapshots* section is used to enable or disable background snapshots. This feature will let snapshots take place in the background so you can still work in VMware Workstation without having to wait for the snapshot status bar to complete. Background snapshots can only be used on VMs that are powered off.

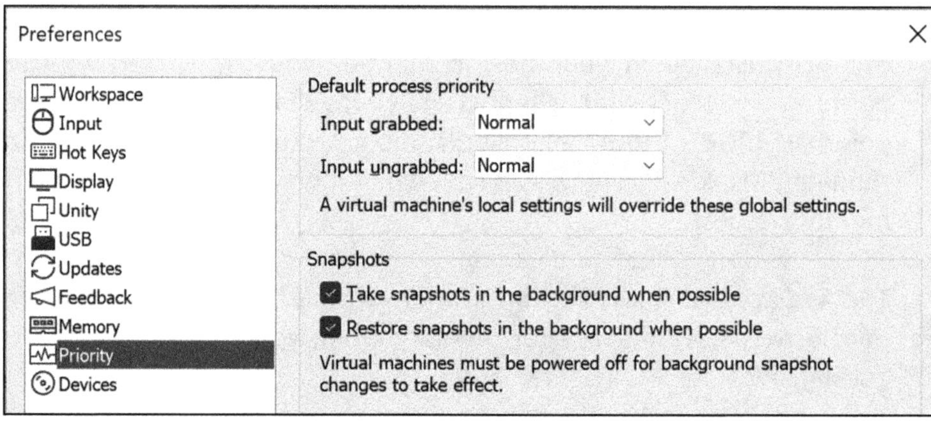

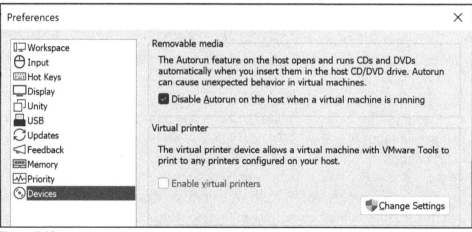

Figure 8.9

- **Devices** – You probably already know that when you insert a CD\DVD or flash drive into your host computer that it will either automatically open it to display its contents or start the installation program if it's that type of media. If you don't want this happening on your virtual machines, you can come here and disable *Autorun*.

  If you would like to have your VMs be able to print to a printer connected to your host computer, then you can come here and enable the virtual printers option by clicking the *Change Settings* button.

Figure 8.10

Unity Mode

If you find yourself going back and forth between your host and guest VM to use specific applications, then you might want to try Unity Mode. This feature allows

Chapter 8 – Preferences & Extras

you to use your guest applications from the desktop of your host. It works by making these guest applications appear to be running on your host even though everything is still taking place on the guest VM.

On my VM I have a PDF file open, a webpage open to the VMware website and my File Explorer app running. Once I click the Unity Mode button in the toolbar, I will see that these three programs running on my virtual machine are now showing on the taskbar of my host along with the programs running on my host PC.

Figure 8.11

When I go back to my VMware Workstation console, I will get a grey screen telling me that I am in Unity Mode and I won't be able to use the virtual machine from the console.

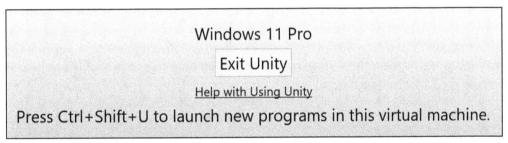

Figure 8.12

When I press Ctrl+Shift+U on my keyboard, I will get a separate start menu for my virtual machine right above the start menu on my host with the name of the VM next to it (figure 8.13).

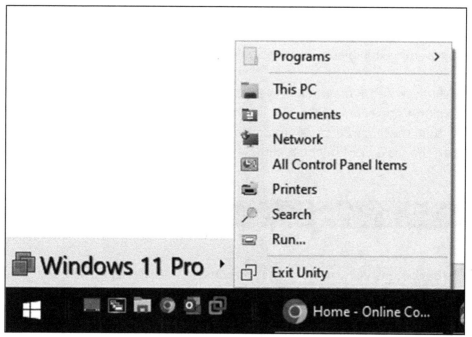

Figure 8.13

If I were to click on *Programs* from this VM start menu, I would see all the installed programs on the virtual machine and be able to run any of them just by clicking on its icon (figure 8.14).

Figure 8.14

127

To exit Unity Mode, I can click on *Exit Unity* from the VM's start menu or go back to the VMware Workstation console and click the Exit Unity button from there.

Mapping Virtual Disks

If you need to access files from a virtual machine or several VMs and don't want to power them on to get to these files, you can simply map a drive on your host to a virtual disk and access the files and folders on that virtual disk directly from your host. If you don't have this option, that is because it was removed from version 17 as of this writing.

To begin the process, make sure the virtual machine is powered off and if it has more than one virtual disk, find the path to the VMDK file you want to access from the virtual machine's settings.

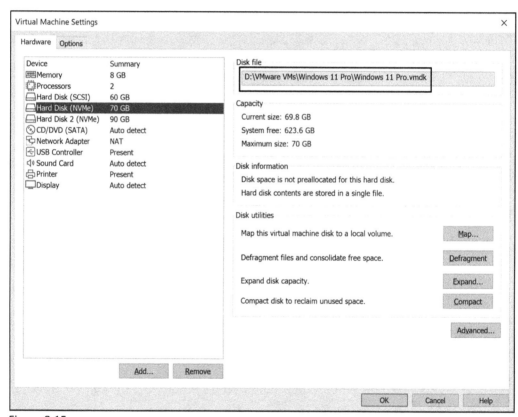

Figure 8.15

Next, you will go to the *File* menu and choose *Map Virtual Disks*. Then you will click on the *Map* button and browse to the location of the VMDK disk file you wish to map.

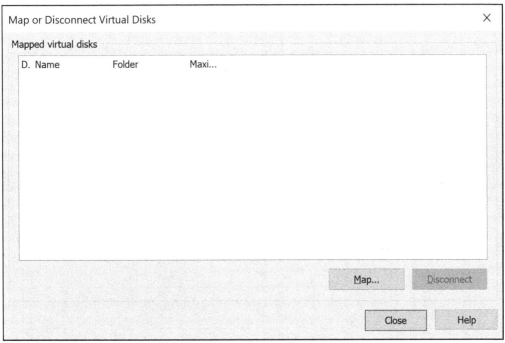

Figure 8.16

If the virtual disk has more than one volume, you will need to select the volume you want to map.

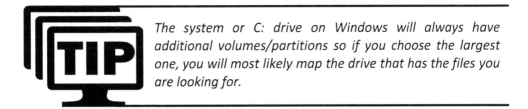

The system or C: drive on Windows will always have additional volumes/partitions so if you choose the largest one, you will most likely map the drive that has the files you are looking for.

I will choose volume 3 since that is the one that will have all of the files that I need to access. You can choose what drive letter you want your host to use for the drive mapping or stick with the default. I will choose V...for virtual. If you leave the box next to *Open drive in Windows Explorer after mapping* checked, it will automatically open your newly mapped drive so you can see its files (figure 8.18).

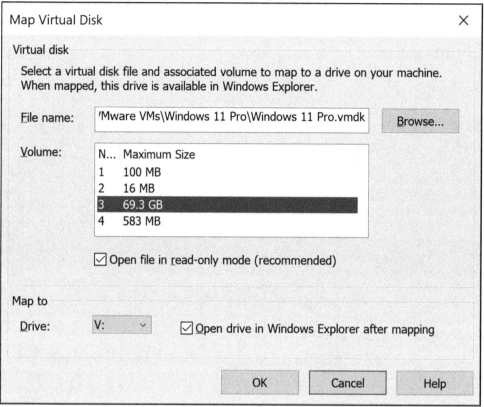

Figure 8.17

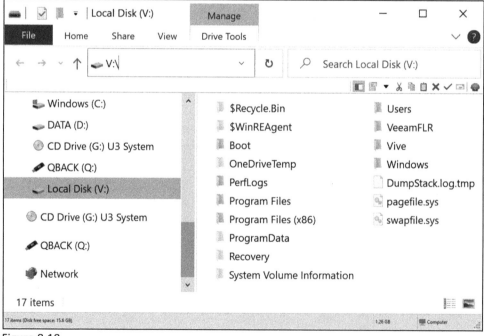

Figure 8.18

Now that the drive is mapped, it shows up under the Mapped virtual disks section. You can then map additional virtual disk drives or click on the *Disconnect* button to unmap the current drive. Just be sure to have any File Explorer windows or other files from the mapped disk closed before doing so, otherwise you will get an error and not be able to disconnect the drive.

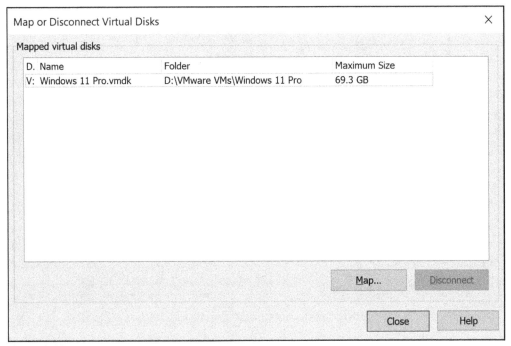

Figure 8.19

Shared Folders
Another way to copy files between your host and guest virtual machines is to use the Shared Folders feature that VMware Workstation offers. By using this method, you can share a folder on your host computer and allow your VMs the ability to access it to get to your files.

On my host computer, I will create a folder called **Shared with VMs** inside of my VMs folder to use for sharing purposes. You can use an existing folder if you like and it can be anywhere on your hard drive.

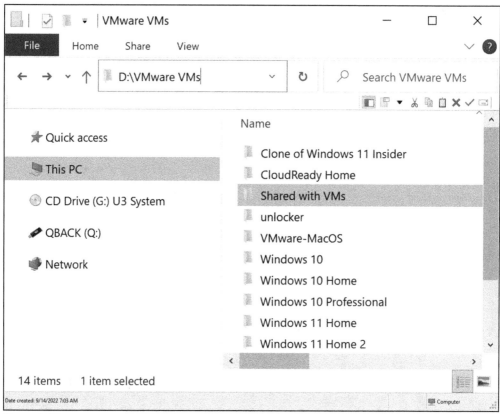

Figure 8.20

Next, you will go to the settings of the virtual machine that you want to be able to access this shared folder. From here, click on the *Options* tab and then on *Shared Folders*.

This feature is disabled by default, and you can have it be always enabled or enabled until you power off or suspend the virtual machine. I will choose the latter. To make the shared folder easier to access, you can check the box that says *Map as a network drive in Windows guests* so your shared folder will have its own drive letter within the VM. Next, I need to add the folder from my host that I want to share by clicking on the *Add* button and browse to its location on my hard drive.

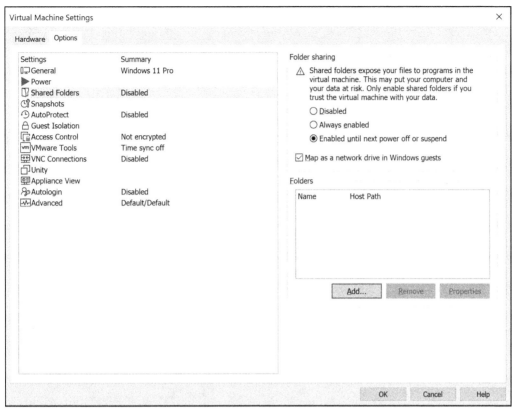

Figure 8.21

Once you find the folder, you will see that it gives the share name the same name as your folder. You can change this name if desired and then click the *Next* button.

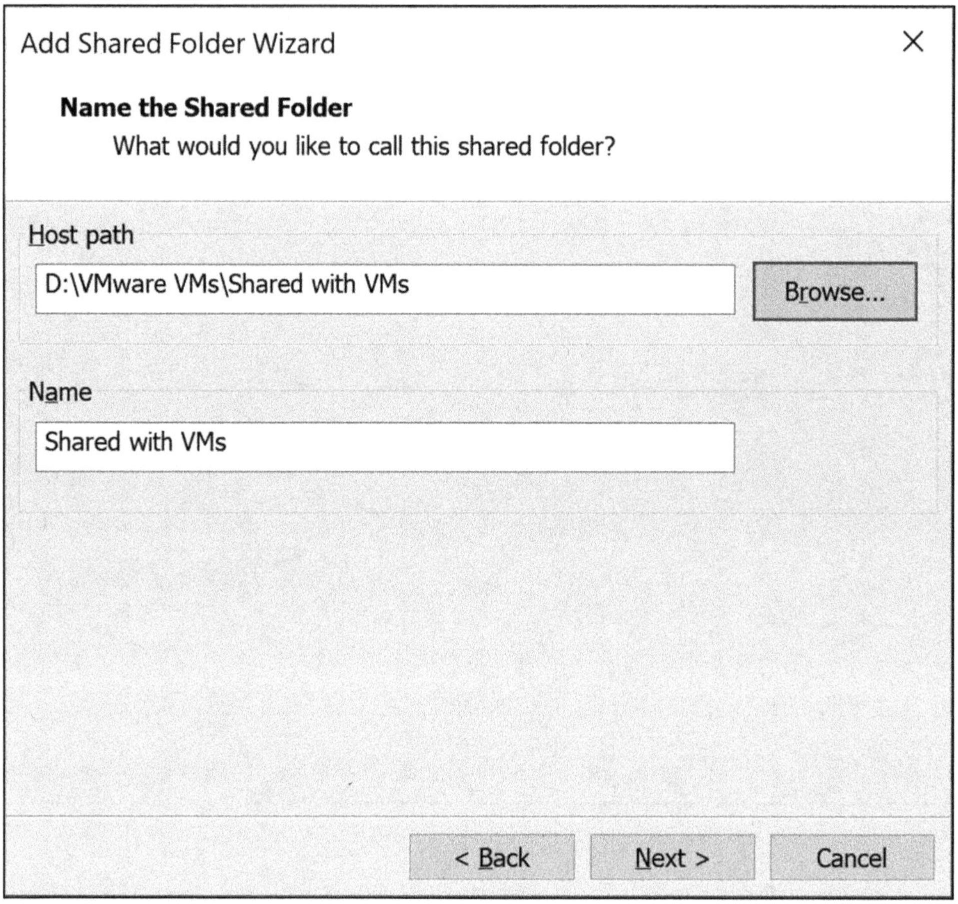

Figure 8.22

You will need to keep the *Enable this share* box checked for this process to work and the *Read-only* box can be used if you don't want any users on your virtual machine to be able to edit or delete your files.

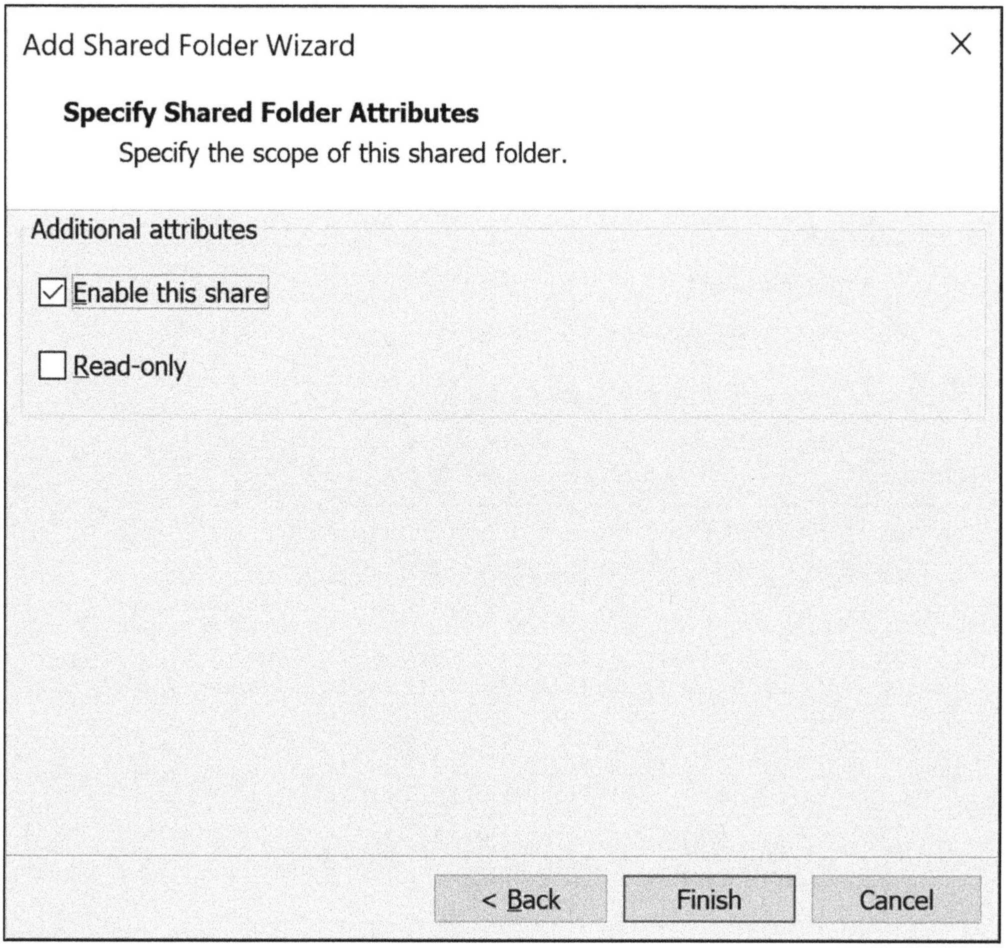

Add Shared Folder Wizard   ✕

Specify Shared Folder Attributes
    Specify the scope of this shared folder.

Additional attributes

☑ Enable this share

☐ Read-only

                              < Back   Finish   Cancel

Figure 8.23

Once you click the *Finish* button, you will see your shared folder listed in the virtual machine's settings. You can then enable or disable this as needed as well as remove the share or add additional shared folders.

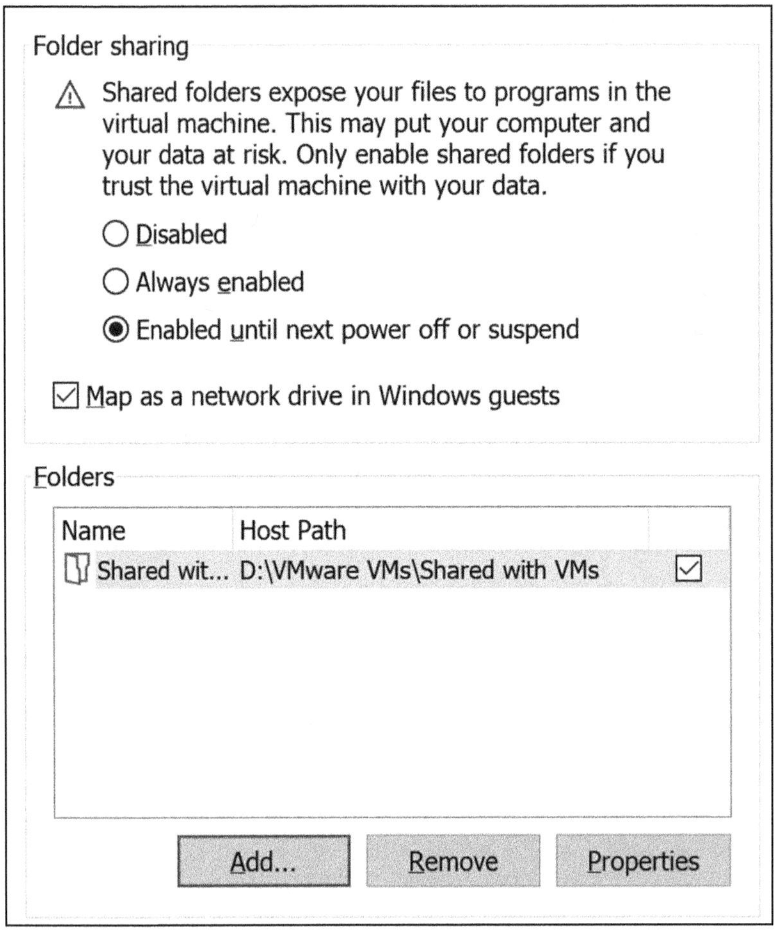

Folder sharing

⚠ Shared folders expose your files to programs in the
virtual machine. This may put your computer and
your data at risk. Only enable shared folders if you
trust the virtual machine with your data.

○ Disabled

○ Always enabled

◉ Enabled until next power off or suspend

☑ Map as a network drive in Windows guests

Folders

Name	Host Path	
🗋 Shared wit...	D:\VMware VMs\Shared with VMs	☑

[Add...]　[Remove]　[Properties]

Figure 8.24

Now when I am on my virtual machine, I can see that shared folder mapped to
my Z drive and can then open the folder and work on the files as needed.

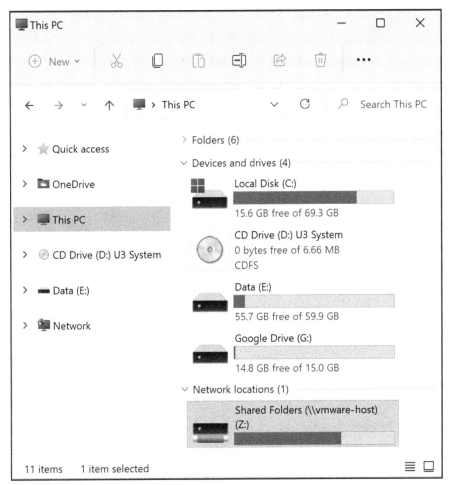

Figure 8.25

Attaching USB Devices

It only makes sense that you should be able to use your USB devices on your virtual machine. If you had a flash drive with some files on it that you needed on your VM, it would be a pain to have to copy them all to your host and then over to your VM or have to share a drive to get this accomplished.

USB access is enabled by default and when you connect a USB device to your host and have a virtual machine running, you will get a popup in VMware Workstation asking you where you would like to use this USB device. You will not be able to access the USB device until you make a decision.

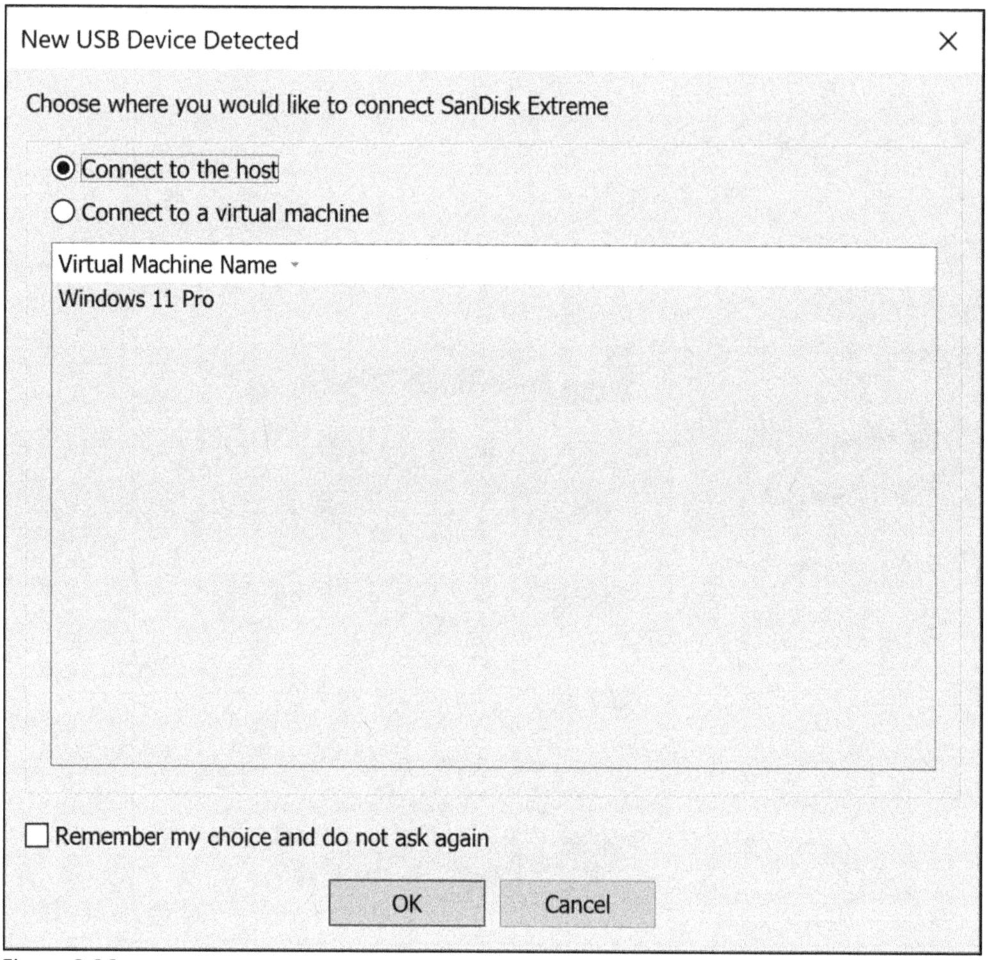

New USB Device Detected   ✕

Choose where you would like to connect SanDisk Extreme

⦿ Connect to the host
◯ Connect to a virtual machine

Virtual Machine Name ▾
Windows 11 Pro

☐ Remember my choice and do not ask again

[OK]　　　[Cancel]

Figure 8.26

If you always want to have your USB device connect to either your host or VM every time, you can make your choice and check the box that says *Remember my choice and do not ask again*.

You can also go into the VMware Workstation preferences and change the option from *Ask me what to do* to one of the other choices (figure 8.27).

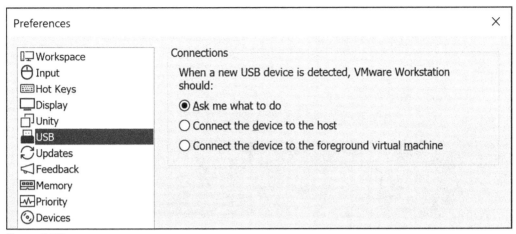
Figure 8.27

If you look at the settings for a specific virtual machine, you can check the USB compatibility and set it to the desired level which will most likely be USB 3.1.

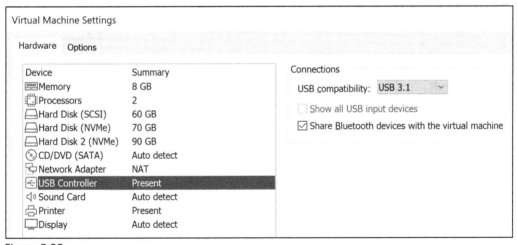
Figure 8.28

Your virtual machines also have the ability to use connected Bluetooth devices and this option is enabled by default.

The checkbox for *Show all USB input devices* is there in case you want to see other devices such as USB mice and keyboards in the status bar which you most likely don't want to see.

The status bar is at the lower right corner of the VMware Workstation window. Here you can see attached devices and their status. If a device is greyed out that means it is not attached and might have been attached before or is now attached to your host and not the VM.

Figure 8.29

You can hover your mouse over an icon to see the name of that device. You can also right click the icon to get options such as connecting or disconnecting the device or as a way to go to its settings.

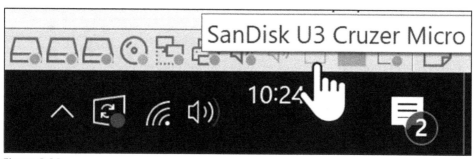

Figure 8.30

Printing

Another commonly used device that you might want to use with your virtual machines is a printer. If you have a printer attached to your host computer, you have the capability to print to it from your virtual machines as if they had it attached locally.

To configure VM printing, you will need to go back to the Workstation preferences and enable the virtual printer by clicking on the *Change Settings* button in the *Devices* category.

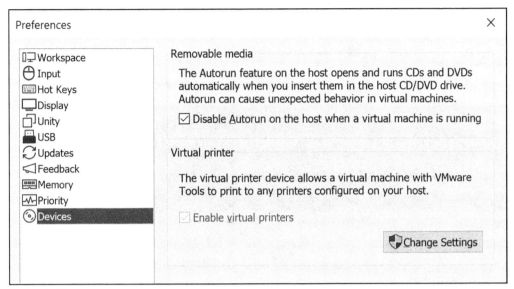

Figure 8.31

Then you will be able to go to the hardware settings for the virtual machine and click the *Add* button and add a printer if you don't have one already configured for you which you most likely will. Just make sure that the *Connected* and *Connect at power on* boxes are checked.

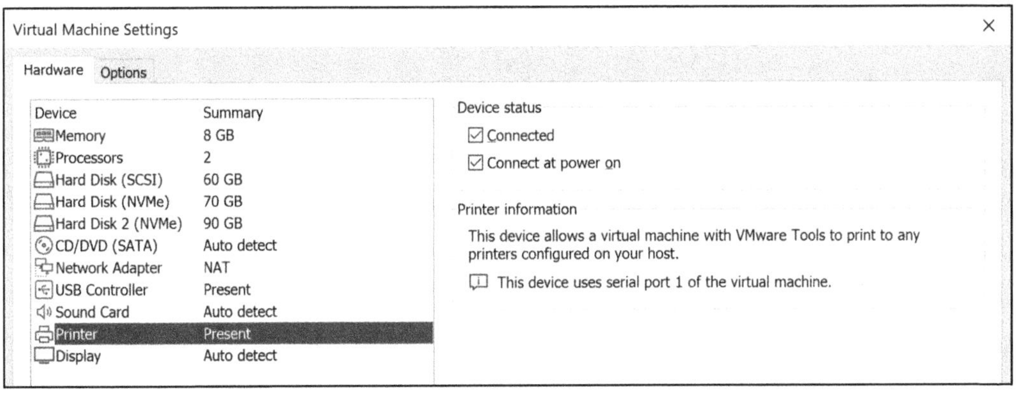

Figure 8.32

You should see a printer icon with a green status light in the Workstation status bar if everything is working. Of course your printer will need to be powered on and properly connected to your host in order to print from your virtual machine. You will also need to install the printer in your guest OS and provide any drivers as needed.

Figure 8.33

Screen Captures

One thing I often have a need to do is take screenshots of open windows or programs on my screen to use for things such as adding illustrations to books. If you are a Windows user, then you probably know you can use the print screen key on your keyboard or even the Windows Snipping tool to capture screenshots of anything on your monitor.

If you want a quick way to capture what is on the console screen of your virtual machine, you can use the screen capture feature from within VMware Workstation.

To do so, open the console for the virtual machine whose screen you want to capture. Then from the VM menu click on *Capture Screen* or you can press *Ctrl-Alt-PrtScn*. You will then get a message saying your screenshot was copied to the Windows clipboard and also saved as a file on your desktop.

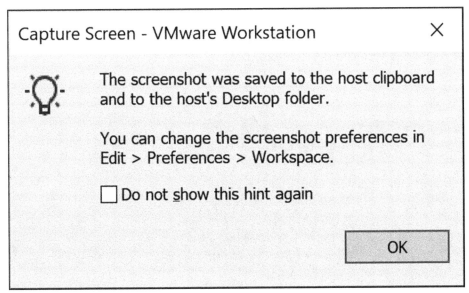

Figure 8.34

Since it was copied to your clipboard, you can then paste the VM screenshot image into a document, email or anywhere else that you can paste images. Figure 8.35 shows an example of a screenshot pasted into a document.

Figure 8.35

You will also have a PNG image file saved to your desktop that you can view or email etc. rather than having to paste your screenshot into another app to save it as a file.

If you want to change the screen capture options, you can go to the VMware Workstation preferences and disable the clipboard option, disable the save as file option or change where the file is saved to.

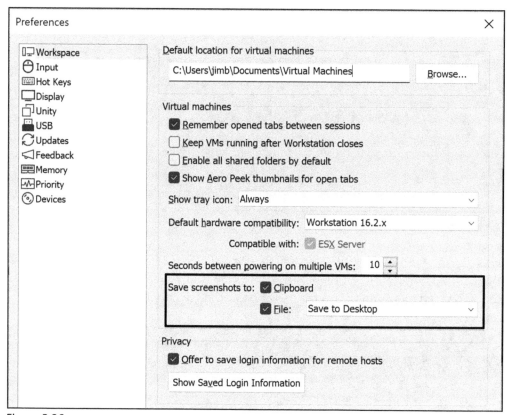

Figure 8.36

Disk Cleanup, Compacting & Defragmenting

Just because your VM hard drives are virtual doesn't mean they don't need occasional maintenance like the physical hard drive in your host computer. VMware Workstation offers several ways to make sure your virtual disks are performing at their best.

Disk Cleanup

As you add files to your virtual machine, the virtual disk will grow along with it assuming you used a dynamic disk. But when you delete files from your VM, you won't necessarily reclaim all of the space that those files were using. This is where a disk cleanup can really help you out.

The disk cleanup feature is used to reclaim space on the virtual disk from files that are no longer used by the guest operating system. The Cleanup disks command operates directly on the virtual disk (.vmdk) files. This process will only work for virtual machines running Windows.

To run the disk cleanup you can go to the VM menu and choose Manage and then *Clean Up Disks*. You will then be shown how much disk space the VM is using and also how much space you will be able to get back from running the cleanup. The virtual machine must be powered off to run this process though.

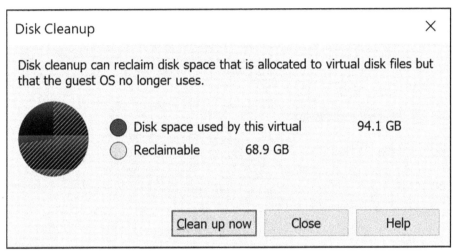

Figure 8.37

After the disk cleanup is complete, you can check it again to see how much space your virtual disks are using after the process.

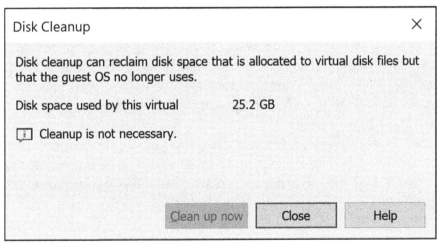

Figure 8.38

Disk Compacting

This is a process that is used to reclaim free disk space kind of like when you compact a database file. Virtual disks can take up more space than they are actually using so this is a way to shrink them down to where they should be.

Once again, the VM must be powered off to run the compact process. You can find this option in the virtual machine's settings for each virtual hard disk. Don't expect to get much space back with this process compared to the disk cleanup method I just discussed.

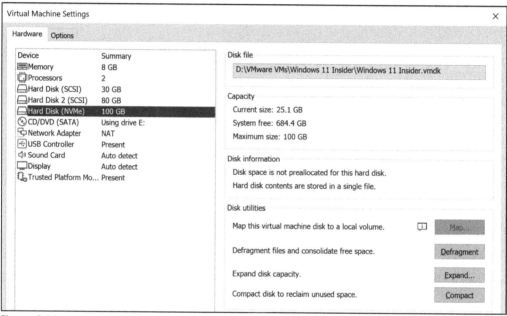

Figure 8.39

Defragmenting Disks

If you have been a Microsoft Windows user for some time, you probably remember the days when we had to "defrag" our hard drives to keep things running smoothly. These days, Windows does this for us and with SSD (solid state) disks, you really don't need to defragment them to begin with.

When a disk becomes fragmented, files and programs get out of order for lack of a better term and the disk does not perform as well as it should. Defragmenting a disk will put everything back in order to increase overall disk performance.

You might eventually see a message similar to figure 8.40 when working in VMware Workstation. And when this happens you can easily defragment the disk from the same area as you go for the compact option (figure 8.39).

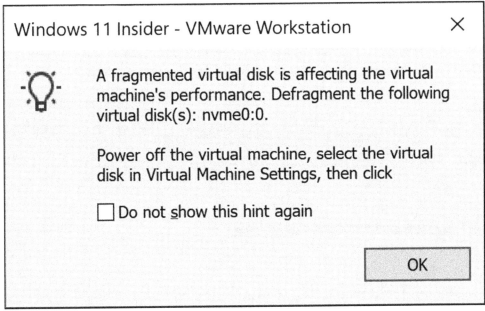

Figure 8.40

In order to run the defragment procedure, the virtual machine will need to be powered off and you will also need enough free space equal to the size of the virtual disk file if your VM is using a single VMDK file.

The defrag process will take some time and will vary depending on the size of your virtual hard disk file, but you will be shown a status bar to give you an idea of the progress.

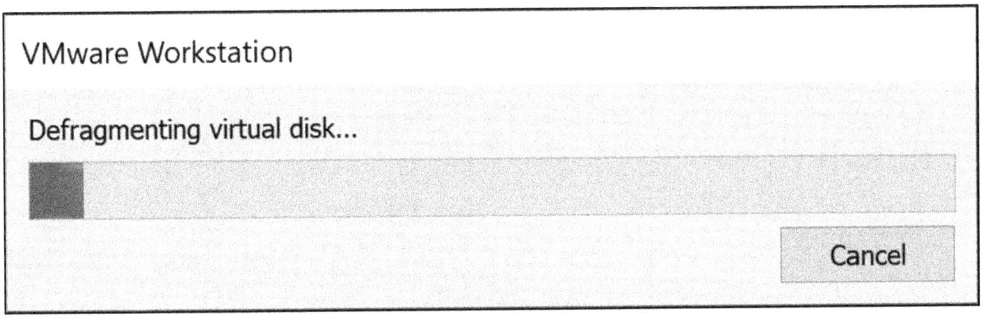

VMware Workstation

Defragmenting virtual disk...

Cancel

Figure 8.41

Encrypting your Virtual Machines

If you share your VMware Workstation environment with other users and don't want them accessing a certain virtual machine, you can encrypt that VM so nobody can use it or change its settings without knowing the encryption password.

To encrypt a VM, go to the virtual machine settings and then to the Options tab. Next, go to the *Access Control* section and click on the *Encrypt* button.

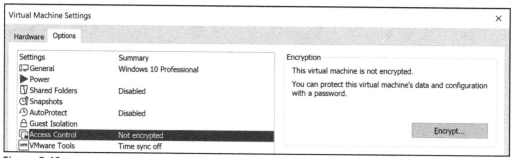

Figure 8.42

You will be prompted to enter a password for the virtual machine. Just be sure to remember this password or write it down because if you forget it, there is no way to recover it.

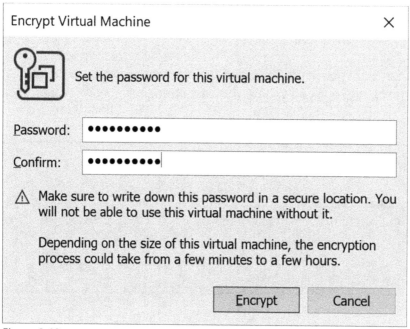

Figure 8.43

The encryption process will take some time so make sure you don't need to work on any virtual machines before starting it.

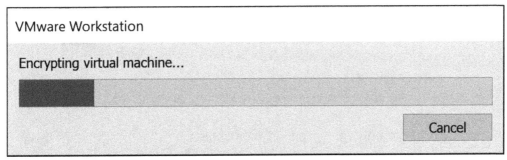

Figure 8.44

Now when you go back to the Access Control section you will have an option to remove the encryption. You will need to enter the password you created in order to do this.

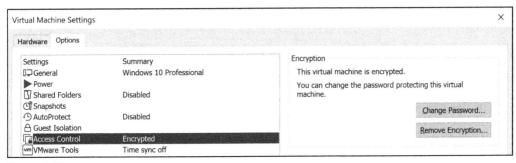

Figure 8.45

When you or anyone else now clicks on the encrypted VM to use it or look at its settings etc., you will get a password box and will have to enter the correct password to continue.

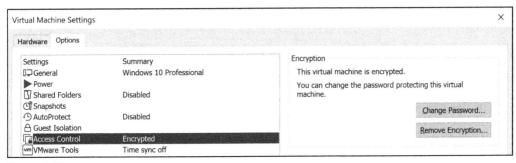

Figure 8.46

There are some limitations that come with encrypting a virtual machine. Here are a few of them.

- You will not be able to manually view or edit any configuration files.

- You cannot create a linked clone from an encrypted virtual machine.

- You cannot encrypt a shared or remote virtual machine.

- You cannot share an encrypted virtual machine.

- You cannot upload an encrypted virtual machine to a remote server.

Disable the Virtual Machine Auto Suspend Feature

Once you start using VMware Workstation for a bit of time you might notice that it will automatically suspend your virtual machines after a certain time of inactivity by you. Then you will have to click on Resume and wait for Workstation to start the VM again. When a virtual machine is suspended, the current state of the operating system and applications is saved, and the virtual machine is put into a suspended mode. This is kind of like when Windows goes into sleep or hibernate mode.

If you want to disable this feature, you can edit the .vmx file for the virtual machine and add a line of text to disable it. This .vmx file is used to hold configuration information for the virtual machine and can be found in the location of your VM files.

If you don't know where your virtual machine files are located, you can go to the VMs settings, click on the Options tab and look in the *Working directory* box.

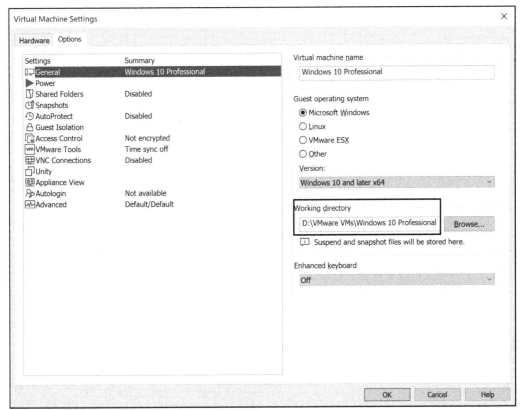

Figure 8.47

Then you can find the .vmx file which will have the name of the virtual machine in front of it such as **Windows 10 Professional.vmx**. Then you can right click on the .vmx file and open it with Notepad or any other text editor you might like to use.

Then at the bottom of the file, add a line that says **suspend.disabled = "TRUE"** and save the file. You will need to reboot the virtual machine to have the changes take effect.

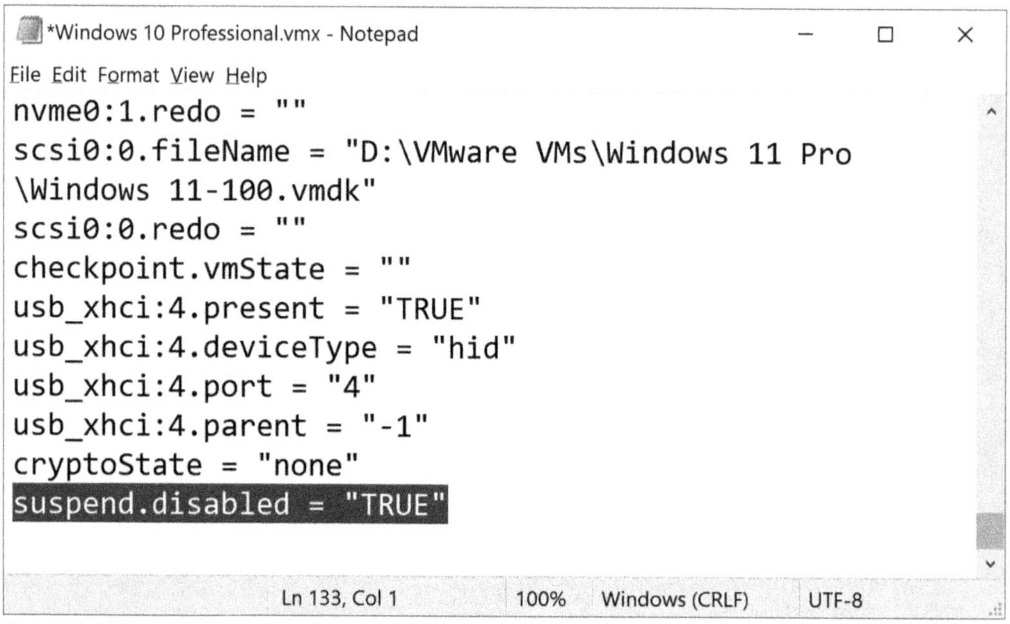

```
*Windows 10 Professional.vmx - Notepad                    —    □    ×
File Edit Format View Help
nvme0:1.redo = ""
scsi0:0.fileName = "D:\VMware VMs\Windows 11 Pro
\Windows 11-100.vmdk"
scsi0:0.redo = ""
checkpoint.vmState = ""
usb_xhci:4.present = "TRUE"
usb_xhci:4.deviceType = "hid"
usb_xhci:4.port = "4"
usb_xhci:4.parent = "-1"
cryptoState = "none"
suspend.disabled = "TRUE"

            Ln 133, Col 1        100%   Windows (CRLF)    UTF-8
```

Figure 8.48

What's Next?

Now that you have read through this book and learned how to create virtual machines and get them working together, you might be wondering what you should do next. Well, that depends on where you want to go. Are you happy with what you have learned, or do you want to further your knowledge on virtualization or even take the next step and learn about enterprise level software such as VMware vSphere or Microsoft Hyper-V? Or maybe learn the free Oracle VirtualBox platform so you can compare it to VMware Workstation.

If you do want to expand your knowledge, then you can look for some more advanced books on virtualization or focus on a specific technology such as cloud platforms, if that's the path you choose to follow. Focus on mastering the basics, and then apply what you have learned when going to more advanced material.

There are many great video resources as well, such as Pluralsight or CBT Nuggets, which offer online subscriptions to training videos of every type imaginable. YouTube is also a great source for instructional videos if you know what to search for.

If you are content with being a proficient VMware Workstation user that knows more than your friends, then just keep on practicing what you have learned. Don't be afraid to poke around with some of the settings and tools that you normally don't use and see if you can figure out what they do without having to research it since learning by doing is the most effective method to gain new skills.

Thanks for reading **VMware Workstation Made Easy**. You can also check out the other books in the Made Easy series for additional computer related information and training. You can get more information on my other books on my Computers Made Easy Book Series website.

https://www.madeeasybookseries.com/

You should also check out my computer tips website, as well as follow it on Facebook to find more information on all kinds of computer topics.

www.onlinecomputertips.com
https://www.facebook.com/OnlineComputerTips/

About the Author

James Bernstein has been working with various companies in the IT field for over 20 years, managing technologies such as SAN and NAS storage, VMware, backups, Windows Servers, Active Directory, DNS, DHCP, Networking, Microsoft Office, Photoshop, Premiere, Exchange, and more.

He has obtained certifications from Microsoft, VMware, CompTIA, ShoreTel, and SNIA, and continues to strive to learn new technologies to further his knowledge on a variety of subjects.

He is also the founder of the website onlinecomputertips.com, which offers its readers valuable information on topics such as Windows, networking, hardware, software, and troubleshooting. James writes much of the content himself and adds new content on a regular basis. The site was started in 2005 and is still going strong today.

www.ingramcontent.com/pod-product-compliance
Lightning Source LLC
LaVergne TN
LVHW081345050326
832903LV00024B/1318